What Your Future Holds And What You Can Do To Change It

"Learn to live in a higher realm of life"

Deborah K. Finley

xulon
PRESS

www.xulonpress.com

Dedication

First of all I'd like to thank my Lord Jesus, for being my Savior, my closest friend, my peace, my strength, my healer, my helper, my confidence and the center of my joy, and for the joy you give that endures in all circumstances. Thank you so much for making it possible to complete this book.

Secondly, I'd like to thank God for my godly grandma. Helen Hooper, my mother's mother. She was like a mother to me and was the godly example that I needed to see. Through her I learned that with God all things are possible. I remember the many times I heard her heart cry out to God, thanking him for his mercy. She was a constant reminder to me that our God is full of mercy, that his mercies are new every morning, and that his mercy endures forever. Yet I still dare to hope when I remember this: The faithful love of the Lord never ends! His mercies never cease. Lamentations 3:21-21 NLT

Next I'd like to thank God for my grandpa, Sam Hooper, my mother's father. He showed me the importance of having a child like faith. I'm sure he still does the old soft shoe in heaven, but now with a much bigger smile on his face. I'm glad that when he's jingling his keys in his pocket that it won't irritate my grandma anymore.

"Truly I say to you, unless you repent, (change, turn about) and become like little children (trusting, lowly, loving and forgiving) Whoever will humble himself therefore and become like this little child (trusting, lowly, loving, forgiving) is the greatest in the kingdom of heaven." Matthew 18:3-4 Amplified

I also want to thank God for using my mother when I was going through that dark time in my life. It amazed me when my mother told me to not give up, just as my grandma would have if she had still been here.

Those who hope in the Lord will renew their strength. Isaiah 40:31

And last but not least, thank you, God, for my special Aunt Sherry. I picture Heaven getting a little brighter upon her arrival. I miss her and her laugh. I'll always remember her loving heart and how she realized the importance of laughter. I'll never forget one of the last verses of the Bible she reminded me of before she went to Heaven. She said, "Remember we love him, because he first loved us." 1 John 4:19

Acknowledgements

First of all I'd like to thank my best friend, favorite Psalmist, wonderful father, and handsome husband Kirk. I love you more each day. Thank you for always encouraging me to get this book finished so I can get on with the next one. Thank you so much for always believing in me and supporting me in word and in prayer and for being so understanding of all the late nights and long days it took for me to complete this book. I don't know what I'd do without you.

Secondly I'd like to thank my Pastor Tim Roames and his wife Leeann for being such a blessing to us in our life.

Next I'd also like to thank Herbert Kirshner, my eighth grade English teacher, for being a positive influence in my life.

My heartfelt thanks to my special friend Violet O'Brien for always being such an encourager and blessing during this time, and for Bob O'Brien, thank you both so much for your prayers and time you took in helping.

Thanks to my editor, Julie Dearyan for being there for me, I will always remember and appreciate the time you took and the wonderful job you did.

Last but not least, I'd like to thank all my family and friends that have been such a blessing to me! I can't find the words to express my gratitude for all your prayers and encouragement so I could complete this. You know who you are.

Contents

Foreword
by Tim Roames

You hold in your hand a book that will encourage you, surprise you, challenge you and guide
you into some truths that will help heal past hurts
and change your future for the better.

Debbie Finley, the author of this excellent book,
<u>What Your Future Holds and What You Can Do
to Change It,</u> is someone I've had the privilege of
knowing for over 27 years and have witnessed her
deep faith in God. Debbie and her husband Kirk
attend the church I pastor and have served on staff
for 6 years. Their lives are certainly an encouragement to all who know them. And their love for God
is evident in all they do.

In this book, Debbie tells her true-life story of
overcoming great hurt and changing her bleak future
into a bright one. Debbie explains how she did it
and shows us, the readers, how we can do the same

thing. Debbie's story is true. The characters really existed and the God she talks about is real. I know you will be blessed as you read this book and apply what you read.

Pastor Tim Roames
Pastor of Good News Christian Center

Des Plaines, IL

Debbie and I have been married now for thirty two years. The first three years we had more downs than ups. Our financial struggles were always a challenge. Then something wonderful happened in our lives, we accepted Jesus Christ as our Lord and Savior. What a difference he made. He changed everything.
We saw each other in a different light. We started understanding his love and forgiveness, and started walking in it. Our love and respect for each other started growing more and more each day, and thirty two years later, it's still growing. Debbie has been through some real tough times in her life.

Through her studying God's word, being led by the Holy Spirit, and acting upon what she has read and learned, she has turned those tough and sometimes very tragic times into victory.

I'm so proud of what God is doing in her life. God has given her the privilege to speak at women shelters, churches, etc. where people have come to realize that things can change from bad to good. He is using her mightily to help others that have been suffering through failure and hard times.

Our prayer is that the God-given insight in this book, his life changing word, will give you hope and inspire you to go for God, have a great life and a great future!

I love you very much, Debbie Kirk

Endorsements

Ithoroughly enjoyed reading Debbie Finley's book

It is an inspirational testament to the miraculous power of faith. Her staunch belief in the Bible has given her life new meaning and purpose. What an amazing transformation from a childhood that threatened to destroy her.

Herb Kirshner,
Debbie's eighth grade English teacher

As I read the words of this book I was reminded of a Scripture in Psalms that says: He sent his word to heal them and delivered them from the pit of destruction. With the power of his word and his great love he takes our shattered lives and restores us. Thank you for letting God use your life and this book to bring hope to many! You go girl! We love you so much!

Beltran and Vera Amador
Missionaries from Oaxaca, Mexico

I truly recommend reading this book. It is definitely God-led and inspiring! Whether you are a believer or not, this book is for you! As you read this book, let the power of God move in you as it did in me. Ask God to open your mind to understand and your heart to receive the blessings and the joy that awaits. The compassion the Lord has given Debbie for people is truly evident. Remember, all God's promises are true!

Rejoice Always, In Jesus name
Evangelist Felicia King
Church of the Apostolic Road
Capron, Il.

Introduction

Have you ever wondered or hoped there could be more to life but thought it was too good to be true?

Have you ever wondered if you had a future?

Have you ever felt that you had no control over what your future held?

Whatever your situation is now, or whatever situation you may have come out of, this can be an opportunity for you to see a change for the better.

This book can help you to see that whatever your circumstances in life may be, no matter how bad it may look, no matter how big the problem may seem . . . things are subject to change. All things are possible to those who believe.

Your future may look very bright, I hope it is, but then again, your future may seem uncertain. Maybe you've heard of the song, "What a difference a day makes, 24 little hours." Sometimes it can be a positive, sometimes a negative. Your health may or may not be a concern. You may be set financially but are very unhappy. Money can't buy you love.

The tabloids are a perfect example of how money can't buy you love and happiness. So many celebrities have a lot of money, but are getting divorced everyday, not once, not twice, but many times, because of love and happiness coming to an end.

What the world needs now is love, sweet love. We need a love that doesn't come to an end. Human love can be selfish, human love can end.

But there is another kind of love that is greater, that never fails, and never comes to an end. As you continue to read, the truth can set you free.

Happiness is the result of happenings, when things good are happening; it makes it easier to be happy.

If things aren't so good it's easier to be unhappy.

Many of these things can determine what your future may look like. It's only natural. Then again things are subject to change when you believe in the supernatural.

There's a big difference between joy and happiness. Happiness is based on circumstances. Joy is deeper than happiness. Joy can remain in spite of your circumstances.

CHAPTER 1

Born to Run for my Life

My mother said I was born feet first, so I was a pain from the beginning. "You cried all the time when you were a baby," she said. "You were so stubborn, I wish I never had children," I don't know why anyone would want to have children!

Words like this don't do much for ones self esteem. I decided to do some research to see if I could find out anything positive. Well, according to statistics/studies, less than 4% of babies are born feet first. It actually states that breech birth is perfectly normal and natural. It is a variation of normal and not to be considered an emergency or dangerous. The baby is in that position for a reason, and he/she knows best. I guess I wanted to hit the ground running. I thought it was kind of interesting when I came across some information on the personality traits of the breech. The breech personality is known to be tough, a survivor, ambitious and tense according to the Association of Birth Psychology and their preliminary research to date. I choose to believe that I was born feet first, because I was born to come out running, running for my life. I was born to run the race, and instead of coming out head first, I had a head start by coming out feet first. Maybe it explains my shoe fetish, and how I need to build another room onto our house for all the shoes I have.

The Race of Life

Now, on a more serious note, I thought about life and how it could be compared to a race. I was reminded of how when you're in a marathon and how on the sidelines there are people cheering you on. Also when you're in a race it is vitally important to be as lightweight as possible. So nothing holds you back or pulls you down. If you were carrying suitcases/baggage, it would hinder your endurance, so you wouldn't be able to keep running.

Many of us are carrying bags along with us in life that are holding us back, that are keeping us from having the freedom to run. We get bogged down with all this weight: bitterness, unforgiveness, hurts, fears, etc. When you think about it, we can learn from the veteran runners in the Bible.

In the book of Hebrews it says we are surrounded by such a great cloud of witnesses, and to throw off everything that hinders and the sin that so easily entangles, and let us run with perseverance the race marked out for us.

It also says to fix our eyes on Jesus, the author and finisher of our faith, who for the joy set before him endured the cross, scorning its shame, and sat down at the right hand of the throne of God.

Maybe you're carrying a bag of guilt, grief, perhaps fear, maybe discouragement, or anger. Whatever is in the bag you're carrying, it's time to let it go.

"Give all your worries and cares to God, for he cares about you." 1 Peter 5:7 NLT

You may think, "But I have a reason to carry this bag of unforgiveness, I have a right." "I'll never forgive him or her." I know that I used to feel that way. I used to feel like it was being tough, like I'll show him. "I have this bitterness and I have a right to it." I didn't realize that by holding onto resentfulness it was affecting me physically and emotionally and using up energy that I could have used to be more productive.

I had so much hatred that I wanted to kill someone and thought that it was really alright. I felt justified, since they killed someone I loved. I thought it was only natural for me to want revenge. If I forgave, or let it go it was "letting the offender off the hook," I thought. I didn't understand that it was crippling me. It made it hard for me to keep running, it slowed me down. It made it difficult to hold my head up. It made me very depressed. I didn't realize that unforgiveness was the problem.

Running Down the Road to Destruction

So I ran down a road that only led to destruction, a road that was so dark, I could not see any hope or chance of there being any future. I've had many challenges in the area of unforgiveness to say the least. Sometimes we can hold onto bitterness for so long that it becomes like a root, and it grows. It actually is like poison and it makes us suffer.

"Look after each other so that none of you fails to receive the grace of God. Watch out that no poisonous root of bitterness grows up to trouble you, corrupting many." Hebrews 12:15 NLT

We can hold onto it for so long, maybe because we don't think there's anything we can do about it or because we think it's natural. Maybe because we decide we'll just have a drink or something to temporarily forget. If we're not careful, we can get so busy in our lives that we don't allow ourselves to slow down which can prevent us from dealing with the issues of the heart. Or we could keep these things in our hearts for so long that it's become a part of us and we think we're alright. Even when someone else may see something's wrong, we'll say I'm fine. We really need to take the time to examine our hearts and see if there are things we need to let go of.

It can be to our advantage in a major way because these things can have a negative impact. They can affect us physically, mentally, emotionally, and spiritually.

According to many doctors, the effects of forgiveness can include improved relationships, physical functioning, and better response to medical and surgical treatments, and so on. A saying that I used to use a lot in life was, "I don't get mad, I get even," but I came across a saying recently that I like better: The only people you should ever want to get even with are those who have helped you. I thought this was a good thought for all of us to ponder.

Some other weights that may entangle us may be addictions, like shopping, sports, videogames, internet surfing, hobbies, etc. They can be time robbers, stealing precious time that we cannot ever get back that can hinder us from leading fuller more productive lives. I was tired of carrying bags of bitterness and resentfulness with me everywhere. It affects your endurance; it makes it too hard to keep running the race of life.

Forgiveness-Webster's New World Dictionary is defined as 1. to give up resentment against or the desire to punish; stop being angry with and 2. to give up all claims to punish or exact penalty for an offense.

WorldNet Dictionary defines it as 1. the act of excusing a mistake or offense and 2. compassionate feelings that support a willingness to forgive. In biblical terms, the Greek word of forgiveness *aphiemi* means "letting go", "to release from an obligation or punishment" or "voluntary cancellation of a debt." Another Greek word *agape* also has the connotation of forgiving love.

Not Weakness but Strength

Some people see forgiveness as a sign of weakness when it actually is an attribute of the strong. When I thought about it, anyone can hold a grudge, that's easy. It takes strength to forgive. I didn't have that kind of strength. It was love and compassion that gave Jesus the drive to keep going and not give up. It was his love and compassion that I needed. God started helping me to see that he wouldn't tell me to forgive if it weren't possible. I finally realized that I needed to learn from the greatest forgiver, Jesus Christ. He didn't only forgive one or two, or a dozen people for doing wrong against him. But he forgave all of humanity.

As we travel down roads in our life we can be quick to blame God for the hard roads that we go down. Maybe we're at a point and time in our life because of choices that we have made years ago. Maybe we could have made better choices that could have resulted in a better road in which we are now traveling.

Maybe we could have made a right turn to get on the right road but because we made a left turn another series of events happened. A lot of times we can put our trust in the wrong things or the wrong people which affects our future.

This is what the Lord says: "Cursed is the one who trusts in man, who depends on flesh for his strength and whose heart turns away from the Lord. But blessed are they that trust in the Lord, whose confidence is in him." Jeremiah 17:5-7 NIV

So many things in life have happened due to decisions and choices that we have made which led us down certain paths. And then again sometimes the road we end up on is the result of decisions and choices others made that we had no control over. Though the road may be rough that we are on, and though it may look like it's a dead end, there is a way out. God made a way. God is full of mercy. We can get off of some of those bumpy roads if we will turn the right way and follow the sign that says yield: Yield to God.

"Don't yield your members as instruments of unrighteousness unto sin: but yield yourselves unto God, as those that are alive from the dead, and your members as instruments of righteousness unto God." Romans 6:13

We may not be able to control the offenses that happen in our lives but we can control how we handle them. Sometimes people think right away that forgiveness means to condone or excuse the wrongs done. That's why so many times we hold onto unforgiveness, especially when you're justice oriented as I have always been. Unfortunately, justice doesn't heal all wounds. And the saying that time heals all wounds is not always true.

He heals the brokenhearted and binds up their wounds. Psalm 147:3 NIV

Also the saying forgive and forget isn't in the Bible either. However, there are many Scriptures that command us to forgive one another. Though we cannot erase events from our memory, we can choose not to dwell on them and ask the Lord to heal the hurts that were caused. As we take the time to immerse ourselves in God's word more than dwelling on the thoughts that come against our minds, we can gain control. Some may think they have no control over their thoughts, but the Bible says differently. The Bible says we're to cast down every evil thought and imagination. Sometimes those thoughts are just our imaginations, and sometimes it's just the enemy trying to take over our mind. You may have thoughts of anger, fear, thoughts of unbelief, thoughts of unworthiness, etc.

"Casting down imaginations, and every high thing that is exalted against the knowledge of God, and bringing every thought into captivity to the obedience of Christ." 2 Corinthians 10:5 ASV

A good example of casting down evil thoughts: When fear has come against me in life, I would speak God's word and thank God for it. I would say, "Thank you Father that you haven't given me a spirit of fear, but of power and of love and a sound mind." This Scripture is found in 2 Timothy 1:7.

"And the peace of God, which surpasses all understanding, will guard your hearts and minds through Christ Jesus." Philippians 4:7 NKJV Then I'd say "Thank you Father that your peace keeps my heart and mind through Christ Jesus." "The Bible says whatsoever things are true, whatsoever things are honorable, whatsoever things are just, whatsoever things are pure, whatsoever things are lovely, whatsoever things are of good report; if there be any virtue, if there be any praise, think on these things." Philippians 4:8 "The things which you both learned, and received, and heard, and seen in me, do and the God of peace shall be with you." Philippians 4:9

How to Replace the Bad with the Good

Just as the saying goes that you need to replace bad habits with good habits. We need to replace our bad thoughts with good thoughts.

Be not conformed to this world but be transformed by the renewing of your mind. Romans 12:2

Set your mind on the things that are above, not on the things that are upon the earth. Colossians 3:2

If we dwell on thoughts that come to us such as how we should take revenge into our own hands our thoughts can overtake us. If we do not get rid of these things in our hearts and replace the bad thoughts in our minds, we may eventually act on those thoughts. If we act on those thoughts there may well be consequences that we suffer from as a result. It can affect our whole course in life by choosing to be or not to be a forgiver.

Choose to be free from unforgiveness. Choose to no longer be a victim by letting go of bitterness. It only hurts yourself to hold on to it. I can tell you from experience and maybe you can say the same thing. If we stay bitter instead of getting better, it can harden our hearts and make us very negative and unpleasant to be around. Don't run from your problems. Run to the one that loves you so much. God is more than willing and able to help you.

"Have mercy on me oh God, according to your unfailing love; Psalm 51:1

The Lord is our helper Hebrews 13:6 NIV

I lift my eyes to the hills, where does my help come from? My help comes from the Lord, the maker of Heaven and earth. Psalm 121:1

God is our refuge and strength, a very present help in times of trouble. Psalm 46:1

Wrong is still wrong regardless whether we forgive the offender. When forgiving, it cannot undo a tragedy but it can undo the effects that it has on you. By changing your old thoughts and attitudes, your whole life can change. You can trade your sorrows for joy, sickness for health, and worry for peace. As the Bible says, "Think on these things: whatever things are lovely, that are of good report, if there is any virtue, if there is any praise, think on these things, whatever you've learned, received or heard from me, or seen in me-put it into practice. And the God of peace will be with you."

I first thought about forgiving from my mind and I said I couldn't. But then I set my will to do God's will by yielding my heart to him. I realized it was a matter of the heart, not the mind. We can say I forgive but they are only empty words if they are not from the heart. And God knows our heart. I'm reminded of the Scripture where Jesus said, "these people show respect with their mouth and honor me with their lips but their heart is far from me." Their worship of me is worth nothing. They teach man made ideas as if they were commands from God." Matthew 15:8. When I drew near to God to ask for his help, he drew near to me and extended his mercy and grace to help heal my wounded heart.

Just as it takes consistent effort to hold angry and hateful thoughts in our minds, it's a conscious decision. You can make a decision to refuse to hold resentment just the same as you decided to hold onto hate and revenge. God started helping me to see that he wouldn't tell me to forgive if it weren't possible. He reminded me that I wasn't alone in this but that he was my helper and strength.

My flesh and my heart may fail, but God is the strength of my heart and my portion forever. Psalm 73:26 NIV

I will love thee, oh Lord, my strength. Psalm 18:1

Supernatural Forgiveness

Though it may not seem natural to forgive, especially when such tragedies such as murder, or sexual abuse, etc. have happened, God is supernatural and when we become one with him, we have his love and his power within us. His love is the greatest power there is. His nature is then imparted to us and as we abide in him, his love abides in us giving us his ability.

He who says he abides in him ought himself also to walk just as he walked. 1 John 2:6 NKJV

We cannot abide in his love and be bitter at the same time.

I believe so many of us can be running in so many directions in our lives and be in such a hurry, when we may subconsciously be avoiding matters in our hearts that need to be dealt with. We run here and run there or do things that may use or waste so much time while ignoring the issues of the heart that are so important. Throughout my life, my way of coping with things was to just block them out and sometimes it does help us cope, but sometimes that's all it does. I dealt with things in that way and that's all it did. It helped me cope.

Just as so many of us do, we may have a drink or two, or use another choice of habit which may help us to cope by blocking things out. As time went on I realized that things needed to be dealt with in order for me to have a better quality life, and in order to be able to be more productive. I'm so thankful that I've learned to run to God. As we run to him, he is waiting with open arms to bring us to himself, to draw us closer. "Draw near to God and he'll draw near to you." James 4:8 "People have children for their pleasure and we were created by God for his pleasure." Revelations 4:20 I always had a hunger for the supernatural as a lot of people do. It's because we were created to have fellowship with a supernatural God. But when your mind is so used to thinking naturally it makes it hard to believe in the supernatural. That's a natural reaction. But as you desire to know God in a more intimate way, and as you seek him you will find that it becomes easy and exciting. God said he would fill those who hunger after him.

Blessed are they that do hunger after righteousness: for they shall be filled. Matthew 5:6 NIV

You will seek me and find me when you seek me with all your heart.

Jeremiah 29:13 NIV

God Loves You

As I came to a better understanding of God's love for me, it made it easy to trust him. When I felt it was hard to believe that God's promises were true, it was because I didn't understand how much he loved me. As I came to understand his unconditional love for me, it became easy and natural to believe in the supernatural.

And now these three remain faith, hope and love. But the greatest of these is love. 1 Corinthians 13:13 NIV

When Paul prayed for the Ephesians he said, "For this cause I bow my knees unto the Father of our Lord Jesus Christ, Of whom the whole family in Heaven and earth is named, That he would grant you, according to the riches of his glory, to be strengthened with might by his Spirit in the inner man; That Christ may dwell in your hearts by faith; that ye, being rooted and grounded in love, May be able to comprehend with all saints what is the breadth, and length, and depth, and height; And to know the love of Christ, which passes knowledge, that ye might be filled with all the fullness of God"

Eph. 3:14-19.

This is my prayer for you.

I pray that our glorious Father, the God of our Lord Jesus Christ, would give you the spirit of wisdom and revelation so you may come to know him more. Ephesians 1:17

To know him is to love him. The more we come to know him the more we love him.

We love him because he first loved us. 1 John 4:9

God's Plan for You

God has a purpose and a plan in this great race of life for you. Are you too tired, and ready to give up? Maybe you've lost that spring in your step and are starting to drag your feet?

When you travel, is it hard for you to travel light? It's always been hard for me. Maybe you can relate. When it comes to shoes, if it weren't a problem, I would like to have a big suitcase just for my shoes. But it can make it difficult when you carry around too many bags. It slows you down.

Give all your cares to God because he cares for you. God is cheering you on. He has the stamina that you need.

Come to me, all you who labor and are heavy-laden and overburdened and I will cause you to rest." I will ease and relieve and refresh your souls.

Matthew11:28 Amplified

We just went through some issues recently regarding flood insurance. We aren't in a flood zone, but were told we needed to get flood insurance anyway until we get certain documentation. It was a little frustrating to say the least.

The Lord reminded me of a great Scripture that we can stand on when the storms of life come against us. "Though the enemy comes in like a flood, the spirit of the Lord will lift up a standard against him." Isaiah 59:19

When I was a new believer I remember how I used to think, "I need more faith. If I only had more faith, then I could believe." But as time went on, I realized that when I got a revelation of God's love, that was what I really needed.

I pray that from his glorious, unlimited resources he will empower you with inner strength through his spirit. Then Christ will make his home in your hearts as you trust in him. Your roots will grow down into God's love and keep you strong. And you may have the power to understand, as all God's people should, how wide, how long, how high and how deep his love is. Then you will be made complete with all the fullness of life and power that comes from God. Ephesians 3:16-19 NLT

Faith in a Loving God

One of my first jobs was working in a restaurant, after a long week of being on my feet for so many days, I went home and laid down, I remember touching my shin bones and how they hurt. I could see and feel little bumps on them underneath my skin and it made me a little concerned. I started thinking about how I should pray but, then I thought, "Do I have enough faith to believe they'll go away?" As I started to pray, God spoke to my heart and said," don't have faith in your faith, have faith in your God that loves you enough and is big enough to heal you." I then realized that he really does love us enough and that by believing he loves us so much it became natural to believe in the supernatural power of God. So I started thanking the Lord that he was my healer and after I praised him for a short time, I looked at my legs and the bumps on my shin bones were gone!

Be not wise in your own eyes; fear the Lord, and turn away from evil. It will be healing to your flesh and refreshment to your bones. Proverbs 3:7-8

O Lord my God, I cried out to you, and you healed me. O Lord, you brought my soul up from the grave; you have kept me alive, that I should not go down to the pit. Psalm 30:2-3 NKJV

Trust in the Lord with all your heart; don't lean to your own understanding. Proverbs 3:5

I am the Lord that heals you. Exodus 15:26

Another time that I was so blessed to learn of and see the supernatural power of God in demonstration, was when my daughter was a baby. She had such a bad diaper rash. Though the doctor gave me an ointment she still had a terrible rash from having diarrhea for days. I felt so bad for her. She was crying and crying because it hurt so much. Her skin was so raw that it started to even spot blood.

The Lord spoke to my heart that I should go and lay my hands on her as it says in the Bible to do: "These signs will follow them that believe, they shall lay hands on the sick and they shall recover." Mark 16:18 As soon as I laid my hands on her, she stopped crying. I could feel the sweet presence of God in her room, she immediately went to sleep. Two hours later, I went to check her and she had new skin. It was so amazing! The rash was completely gone! Her next diaper showed a regular bowel movement and she was fine. That was one of my first experiences of seeing a miracle happen by God through my laying hands on someone. I will never forget that day!

The Lord is faithful to all his promises and loving toward all he has made. Ephesians 1:17

I'm so thankful that God cares about healing for our bodies as well as our emotions and spirits. All God's acts are just and true Daniel 4:37 NLT

We can do all things through Christ that strengthens us. Philippians 4:13

Some religions teach that healing isn't for today. I'm so glad that they are wrong. The Bible says different. Hebrews 13:8 states Jesus is the same yesterday, today, and forever. He healed yesterday, he heals today and forever.

Set Free

When I thought about how I had laid my hands on my daughter and prayed and immediately she stopped crying and went right to sleep, it reminded me of the Scripture in Luke 13:13. A woman who had been crippled by a spirit for fifteen years was bent over and couldn't straighten up at all. When Jesus saw her, he called her forward and said to her, "Woman, you are set free from your infirmity." Then he put his hands on her, and immediately she straightened up and praised God. Of course the woman being crippled for eighteen years is not comparable to my daughter's diaper rash but the moment I laid my hands on my daughter, she immediately stopped crying and fell asleep instantly and she was healed. Malachi 3:6 says, "I am the Lord, I change not."

According to the Bible the disciples were sent out to heal the sick. And when he had called his twelve disciples to him, he gave them power over unclean spirits, to cast them out, and to heal all kinds of sicknesses and all kinds of disease.

Jesus said, "If you continue in my word, you truly are my disciples and you will know the truth and the truth will set you free." John 8:31-32

In Mark 16:15-18 Jesus gives believers authority over evil spirits: And these signs follow them that believe. They shall lay hands on the sick and they shall recover.

Some people might say they don't believe in that. Well, the Bible says these signs will follow those who do believe.

Stretch out your hand to heal and perform miraculous signs and wonders through the name of your holy servant Jesus. Acts 4:30

These are just a few of the Scriptures that reveal the truth. I can't help but be reminded of the Apostle Paul's writings. "People will be lovers of themselves, lovers of money, boastful, proud, abusive, disobedient to their parents, ungrateful, unholy, without love, unforgiving, slanderous, without self-control, brutal, not lovers of the good, treacherous, rash, conceited, lovers of pleasure rather than lovers of God- **having a form of godliness but denying its power. Have nothing to do with them**." 2Timothy 3:2-5 NIV

Don't forget, God loves you. He wants you to be healed from all your past hurts and present distresses. He wants to give you his supernatural strength so you can forgive those who have wronged you. As you discover more about my own journey, I pray you will find grace and strength for whatever you're facing right now.

Debbie at the age of three

CHAPTER 2

Against All Odds

Everybody's got a story. This is a story of a little girl that though all the odds were stacked against her, she did more than survived. She overcame insurmountable obstacles. As she was growing up, she walked in darkness, and it looked like the darkness was going to overtake her. Love broke through that darkness so she could finally see. A price was paid for her freedom and she wants you to know that no matter how bad or how hard life can be, no matter how bleak your future may look, you can have a future with God.

The God of Restoration

You may think it's too late, but as I always say, better later than never. God is a God of restoration. As you read my story I believe it will help you to understand that forgiveness is not a feeling or an emotion but a choice. She was three years old and it was early morning. She was awakened by the sounds of voices in the next room, it sounded like her mom and dad. She could tell they were trying to hold their voices down so not to wake her. She tried to listen, but they were talking so softly that it was hard to make out their words. She sensed that there was something wrong. As she strained to hear, it sounded like she heard her dad say that he was sorry… She heard the front door slam.

Jumping out of bed quickly, she ran to the window. She saw her father walking down the street with a suitcase in each hand. "Where was he going?" she thought. She ran into the kitchen. "Mommy" Where's daddy?" she asked.

"He's gone, and he won't be coming back", she replied.

Debbie ran to her room, and threw herself onto her bed as she cried herself to sleep. How could she be so mean, to make him go away? I heard him say that he was sorry? All I knew was that the one person that showed me such love was taken away from me and I was so hurt. I wasn't old enough to understand. All I understood was that I was bitter at my mother for making him leave. I kept this hurt bottled up inside me and became very withdrawn. A year went by and still, all I could think about was how much I missed my daddy. I had dreams of seeing him again and wondered if they would ever come true. I was so mad at my mother, to the point that when she spanked me, I refused to cry.

I refused to give her the satisfaction of show-ing emotion. I was not old enough to understand that there could be a reason why she sent him away. When I grew older my mother told me that my dad was a big gambler, that he didn't have a regular job, and that he was in the organization and did bad things. I refused to believe it.

I knew my father was good. He was always good to me. He showed love to me that she didn't, why should I believe her? I admired my father so much and to hear her talk against him made me more upset with her. In my eyes, my father could do no wrong. I was crushed. How could I accept it? Especially when he was the one that showed me the love I needed so desperately. A year later my mother met another man named Gene. She went out with him a few times and he took us out for lunch one day. He seemed nice. I was four years old now. My mother said, "Debbie, hurry up," grab your bag, you're going to grandma's house for a few days. I was so excited that I would be staying there. As I skipped up her front sidewalk, I breathed in deeply to smell the wonderful fragrance of the lilac tree in front of her house. It always smelled so good! My grandma always made me feel so special and loved so I was always happy to see her.

I could hear my grandpa in his room counting his money. He'd always leave the door open a little so I could see him. "Come on in, he'd say." Then he would show me all the quarters that he had and the half dollars. You could tell he felt very important and proud of all his coin collections. He gave me some pennies and I knew just what I was going to do with them.

The Candy Store

There was a candy store on the corner of Clark and Roscoe Street called Maxis. Every morning I would get up before anyone else and run across the street to the candy store. I would be anxiously waiting outside the door for the store to open. I wanted to make sure that I got there before anyone else because I wanted to get the winner. There were only one or two winners in the gumball machine. Winners were striped gumballs that you could redeem for a free candy bar of your choice. I would dream every night of winning and sometimes I was lucky enough that I did. Every day I looked forward to trying my luck again. It was the highlight of my day. It was what I lived for. No matter how many times I was disappointed I believed tomorrow I had another chance. I was determined to win.

My real dream was that I would see my dad again one day, and I hoped and prayed everyday that it would come true.

When my mother returned I was unpleasantly surprised because she told me that she married Gene. She could tell I wasn't sure what that meant, so then she said," He'll be coming home to live with us."

She said that it would be nice if I would call him Dad, and that I could think about it. I was very uncomfortable about the whole thing. It was scary for me to think that a stranger would be living with us now. He seemed nice at first but I didn't feel like I could trust him. Gene would feed the squirrels every morning and he showed me a special way to tap the nut on the ground by scratching it back and forth.

The sound would attract the squirrel to come up to him and eat right out of his hand. I tried it and it came and ate out of my hand also. I was surprised that it worked for me. I felt like I had learned a secret. He also bought and cared for flowers and plants that he placed on our window ledge in our apartment, so it appeared that he was a gentle man.

Since my father was gone, I thought it would be nice to have a father figure. Our first Christmas together was nice; it was good to see my mother happy. I got the red fire truck pedal car with the bell and removable ladders on the sides that I always wanted. It even had a monkey in it! I was a little disappointed that the monkey wasn't real though. I remember how I didn't believe there was a Santa, until that night. While my mother, Gene and I were at restaurant one night, he had given someone the key to our apartment and they delivered the fire truck and put the present under the tree, so when we returned I was so surprised and convinced that there really was a Santa. It wasn't long after that that Dr. Jekyll and Mr. Hyde started coming out.

Terrible Evening

One night I awoke to the sounds of my mother screaming, crying and pleading in the next room. When I got up and saw Gene beating her, I told him to stop. He threatened me and made me go back to my room. How could I go to sleep hearing her screaming for help? It was so very hard. I heard her running and him chasing her, as the sounds of things were falling and breaking along the way. She ran out the back door.

As the door closed behind her, I heard Gene screaming as his arm went through the glass of the window at the top of the door. The next morning he blamed her that he had to get so many stitches in his arm resulting in more tension in the house. It wasn't uncommon to wake up to blood on the walls and glass broken everywhere.

My father came here from Greece at the age of sixteen

Seeing My Dad

It had been a year now since I saw my dad. I wondered if I would ever see him again. I really missed him and kept dreaming and hoping that I'd see him again. The following week was my fifth birthday and I was in the school yard when a car pulled up in front. Two men got out and walked up to the school yard fence. At first, I didn't recognize them. They called my name and as I ran closer I realized it was my father with a friend. I was so happy to see him! My dream had come true! What a great birthday present! My mother wasn't too happy about him going behind her back to see me and said I couldn't see him anymore at first. Because of the fact that he was from Greece, she was concerned. She said that she heard of children being kidnapped and never being seen again. I begged her to please let me see my dad and when she saw how much happier I was after seeing him, she agreed to me seeing him on Sundays. I would meet him at my grandmas' house and wait for him to pick me up there. I would watch at the window for him, though he didn't always come as planned. His work required traveling that sometimes got in the way of our visits. When he did come he would always take me out to a nice restaurant. The first thing he would do after he sat down at the table was to wipe his silverware off with his napkin and then tell me to order a steak. At first I had a hard time understanding my dad because he had a very strong Greek accent. I felt bad that I had to say what, so many times to him so sometimes I would just smile and nod as if I understood him to save his feelings. It really made me feel bad though because I wanted to understand everything he said. As time went on I got used to his accent and I would hang onto every word. My father took me to Greek Town often because he knew how much I loved Greek food. I really admired my dads' smile. He even smiled with his eyes. He reminded me so much of Robert De Niro when I was little, especially when he smiled. He resembled him so much that when I saw one of Robert De Niros first movies, it spooked me.

My dad always dressed so sharp in nice suits all the time. Everyone seemed to know him and treated him with a lot of respect wherever we went. I felt proud to be his daughter. It made me feel important because we would always get the special treatment as soon as we arrived. He would also take me to the Chicago Theatre downtown to watch John Wayne movies. I really found John Wayne to be boring but I enjoyed watching my dad enjoy the movies. I liked to be with my dad and it was so nice to know he liked to be with me. He promised me he would take me to Greece some day! I knew I was safe when I was with him.

I dreaded going back home to my mom and stepfather. My mother never was an affectionate person, and now with Gene in the picture it got even worse. When I got home from school, my mother would be getting ready for work and as she would be putting on her makeup I would try to talk to her about my day. Gene would always tell me to leave her alone, or she would say, "Shhh, he'll get mad if he knows you're in here or sees us talking." I didn't want to cause a problem so I just didn't talk anymore. It was very lonely. I could go on and on with the different episodes that happened weekly. Many times after a horrific evening of fear and violence, by morning Gene would apologize. "It won't happen again," he'd say. "Now get dressed, we're going to the zoo!" Like we should be happy and excited and just forget about what happened the night before. He would have us stand in front of the green house where he loved the beautiful flowers. "Why aren't you smiling?" he asked as he took our photograph He would put our photos in a book to make it look like we were a normal family. Really, though, at my age, how did I know what normal was? Every payday, Gene would stop at the bar on his way home. He usually would be out all night when it was payday because then he had the money to buy everyone rounds. Everyone thought he was so nice since he fed the squirrels and all. Sometimes on the way home he would be thoughtful enough to stop at the store. He would go shopping at night when the stores were closed. That time was convenient since he didn't have money left to buy groceries for us. He would come home with cardboard trays with can goods and peanut butter and jelly. I couldn't understand why he didn't splurge a little, especially since he didn't have to pay for it. It really got me upset that he didn't bring us home a nice steak or something. He would laugh, and tell us how he just broke the window and just walked right in. Officer Friendly would visit us often. Sometimes, I would even get to visit Gene in jail. Unfortunately, when he did go to jail, he was usually out the same day, if not by the next day.

We lived in constant fear, never knowing what each day or night may hold. I would go to my room and close the door because I felt so bad about every-thing. My cat, Bootsie, would always come snuggle by me. It was like he sensed when I needed consol-ing. He was a very smart cat. When he wanted to go out, it would open the screen door himself, and when it wanted back in he would open the door by himself. I'll never forget about the time when we had a little puppy and kept it in a big box. My mother would go to calm it when it would cry, by putting her hand in the box. The cat would go to the box at the same time and make the same motion my mom did with its paw. It was pretty amazing!

One day my stepfather's sister was over with her husband and children. Their little girl walked past the TV, and the cat was underneath it. The cat put its paw out as she walked past and scratched her leg. It was a very small scratch, it didn't bleed or anything. The next thing I knew my stepfather and his brother in law were on the back porch with a beer in one hand and a brick in the other to kill my cat with. I was heart broken. I begged my mom to stop them but she wouldn't. Maybe she couldn't for fear of being harmed herself. Of course, at the time I didn't think that way. When Gene saw how it made me cry, he apologized for killing my cat and said he would get me another one. I said I didn't want another one.

Freedom for a Few Days

There were many times that the police came and would handcuff my stepfather and take him away. It was so nice when he was away for a few days. We dreaded him coming back. One day the police came and took him away and he didn't come back for a long time. I was seven years old then, and was so glad that he wasn't coming back. My mother was pregnant with his first son, then. When she visited Gene in prison, she took me with. I can still remember the loud clang of the doors locking behind us as we walked in. It was very dark and cold. She divorced him a year after he was in prison. She was afraid of the day he would come out. Four years went by and he was released. He told her that he had changed and asked her to please give him another chance and remarry him. Unfortunately, she did remarry him and unfortunately, he hadn't changed.

By this time I was twelve years old and my half brother was five. My mother became pregnant again with his second son.

I felt so bad for my brother because when his father was in prison, children at school would ridicule him for it. And now his father came back from prison, but was very abusive, physically and mentally. At the dinner table, if my brother dropped his fork on the floor, he would get knocked upside the head for it. Then he would be told to turn on the light and before he was given the chance to do it, he would be knocked down, and yelled at for not getting there quick enough. We were not even allowed to talk at the dinner table. At the age of four or five, my brother would be told constantly, "You've got to be tough". His father bought a punching bag and would make him punch it continually late at night until he would cry because he was so tired. Then he was told to punch his fathers' hands over and over. Then Gene would shave my brothers' head, and tape the hair to his chest and think it was cute and take a picture of him. I felt so bad for him.

Alone with my Stepfather

This time around my mother worked nights, so we were left alone with my stepfather more often. One night after Gene had a few beers he decided to take us to Lake Michigan. He told us all the way there how he planned to throw my brother in the lake off the rocks so he could learn to swim. We were so afraid. When we arrived, he put my brother on his back and dove in. He kept pushing my brother away as he tried to latch onto my stepfather. All I could do was cry and hope that he wouldn't drown. Thank God he didn't. At home when I would walk from one room to another, I was afraid because if I showed any kind of expression I was told it was wrong. If there were ever a smile, he'd say wipe that smirk off your face before I crack you one. If

I looked serious, he would say, what's wrong with you? Don't look at me like that, like I was disrespectful, and threaten me.

Fear was always in the air. It was rare that we were able to watch anything on TV. Every evening when Gene came home from work he would watch the news and Perry Mason. It was very boring. If Gene came home late from work, there were rare cases that we were allowed to watch something, perhaps funny. It was so nice to laugh. But my mother would get mad at me if I laughed and say it's not funny, it's stupid. I was so bound by fear of what people thought of me from having such low self esteem. When I was in public, if I felt like I might laugh, I would try my best to hold it in. If laughter started to come out, I feared the embarrassment of someone hearing me. Since I was always put down, I feared others would treat me the same.

The negativity was unbearable. If my mother was sick, I would say," I hope you're feeling better" and she would get mad at me for it. She would look at me with hate, like I was being hateful, and say, why do you say that? You know I'll never feel better! As if I was the one being mean. She was so negative, I remember at the age of thirty, she said, she was old and probably wouldn't be alive by next year. If I said she wasn't old, she would tell Gene that I was disrespectful and I was punished with a belt. I would get so mad at her for being so negative all the time.

The Guilt Trip

My mother would continually try to lay guilt on us and try to control us by saying that she probably won't be alive next year. She'd say things like, "You should come over and clean my oven for me". I went to my mother's house and cleaned her oven for her when I was married with children all the time. She did this for fifty seven years. Looking back, I can understand how she felt old at thirty because she had been through a lot. I can remember feeling like I was thirty at the age of sixteen from going through so much myself. She always said I wasn't good enough, as I was growing up. She said "Why can't you be like so and so, they clean the house so great?" If I said there were two of them and they didn't have two brothers to take care of, she would just act like she didn't hear me and continue to go on about how the house is so spotless when they clean.

When we bought her a present, with the little money we had, she would always say something to imply we were cheap and selfish because we didn't buy her something better. If she wasn't telling me how bad I was, she was on the telephone telling others to make me feel even worse so I would feel that not only she felt that way but that everyone else did too. Though there was physical abuse it was more mental abuse with me. When I would come home from school, Gene would ask me questions that I didn't have answers to. Then he would laugh to humiliate me. He said, "How are you going to ever amount to anything? Though he did say since

I had long fingers, I would probably be a good pick pocket some day. I'm glad that I picked up the guitar instead. My self esteem was so low from the mental abuse. I was constantly bombarded with loud thoughts that echoed in my mind of unworthiness. I was afraid to express myself since I wasn't ever allowed to at home. As time went on and I started to get older and see that other people weren't being treated anything like I had been, I wanted to run away. I recalled seeing movies on TV where children were in an orphanage and thought about how nice it would if I were able to go to a place like that.

When I would tell my mom how I felt, she would just act nonchalant and say, "Oh, it's not so bad. If you complain to the authorities and are put in a foster home you could be treated a lot worse from other people. At least you don't get burned with cigarettes."

At some of those places, they do that kind of thing. And then I thought she might have a point there, since she's older, maybe she's right. I decided I'd look at the bright side and be glad that at least I didn't get burned with cigarettes.

My mother did tell me that my grandma wanted to adopt me when I was younger. It made me feel so good that my grandma loved me that much.

When my mother saw my reaction, she made sure to tell me that it wasn't because my grandma loved me. She wanted to adopt me so her daughter would have me to play with. Whenever anyone showed me love, she would tell me something bad about them. I didn't usually believe her but it made me feel bad that she tried to make me feel bad.

I felt that my mother didn't want to give me up because I watched her sons everyday, did stacks of dishes every night, and cooked most of the time, did laundry, etc. When I did get to go outside I had to bring my brothers with me everywhere I went. I watched my brothers so much, that some people thought one of them was my child. I felt like I could hardly take it anymore. I lived in constant fear, never knowing what each day or night may hold. It was very depressing. The responsibility was just too much at twelve years old, on top of all the fear of what tomorrow might bring. It was very difficult to get my homework done while being a referee for my brothers everyday after school.

Even on weekends while everyone else was sleeping, I would be up late washing stacks and stacks of dishes. In spite of my circumstances I did like to sing and sometimes singing songs would help me get through the stacks of dishes. While my friends were out playing softball, I was paying the bills and walking blocks to the Laundromat to wash laundry for our family of five. I finally cried to my grandma one day and begged her to please talk to my mom and tell her I need to have some time to go out with my friends. I needed some time to myself, with a break from the responsibilities of watching my brothers, plus everything else I had to do.

Not a Vacation

My mother talked to my stepfather, and he decided I should stay by his sister's house in Round Lake. He said she had two daughters I could play with and that they live by a lake so we could go swimming. They said I could go stay there for two weeks as a little vacation. The plans were made. Gene's brother in law was picking me up that evening. Gene's sister's husband came to pick me up to take me back to his house in Round Lake. I climbed up into his van, and he handed me my little puppy that I was surprised I was able to bring with. I was so happy that my puppy was coming along with me. As we drove along the dark country roads, I felt afraid. There were no houses in sight and it was pitch black.

As we were driving my uncle asked, "Did you bring a swim suit with you? Yes, I said.

"What kind is it, is it a two piece, or a one piece?"

"A two piece, I said.

"Oh, good, that's what everyone is wearing."

"Why don't you try it on, you can try it on in the back of the van while I'm driving and show me how it looks?"

I hesitated.

"Come on, no one will be able to see you"

"No, I said, I don't want to."

"Oh, come on", he said, I'm your Uncle."

"Then why don't you act like it, I said"

He got quiet, then he pulled over and stopped the van. "Take off your clothes" he demanded, as he reached for me.

Somehow, I kicked him in the chest really hard and he went flying from one side of the van to the other. I was so afraid but I got the van door open and jumped out. I fell into a ditch but still had my little dog. Somehow my little dog made me feel like I wasn't completely alone. Ted jumped out too, he seemed to sober up a little and was disappointed that I wasn't willing to cooperate with his plan. Then he apologized. "Please get back in the van, he said. "I won't do it again. Don't tell anyone this happened."

I had no choice but to get back in, there was nowhere else for me to go. It was all country roads, completely dark and desolate. Since I had nowhere to go, all I could do was hope he meant it and get back in the van.

We drove for about a half hour more, then he pulled over again and tried once again. I started crying and yelling at him while fighting him with all I had. It was a miracle that nothing happened, it was a close call. He finally stopped and said he was sorry again, he was really sorry that I wasn't cooperative. He threatened me, and said if I tell anyone what happened that he would come after me, and that they wouldn't believe me anyway. It was very scary. When we arrived at his house, I was afraid to tell anyone. I really didn't know his wife or children.

I was tempted to tell his daughter one day as we went for a walk, but I didn't. When I received a call from home to see if I was having fun, Ted would peak around the corner and glare at me as if to say I'd better not say anything. I dreaded the ride back home to Chicago with him. On the way back, I was afraid he would try something again. He kept telling me I better not tell anyone what happened or he would come back for me the next day.

I was afraid but when I got home, I did tell my mom. She told Gene and he called and yelled at Ted. The next day was a Saturday morning, and sure enough, I was watching cartoons, and I heard someone banging on the back door yelling my name, it was him. I couldn't believe it. It was so weird. He finally went away, but I always wondered if someday when I was outside walking down the street, if he would be in town and come after me.

Occasional Kindness

There were two times my stepfather was very kind to me. At the age of fourteen, I went out with some friends. I got drunk for my first time. I was so drunk that two people had to bring me home and help me up the stairs. When my stepfather answered the door and saw how drunk I was, he was kind. He didn't yell at me, or even punish me. He helped me to bed and didn't tell my mother. He seemed nicer to me after that like we had bonded or something. He even told my brothers to keep it down the next morning for my hangover's sake.

The other time was when I was being bullied by a girl at school. I was a freshman. She would knock my books out of my hands in the hallway all the time, and throw gum in my hair during class. She was always threatening me. My stepfather said I should break her nose and that then she would quit bothering me. One day she started shoving me and knocking me down. In self defense I did break her nose, and it did work. She didn't bother me anymore. He did help us in the area of being tough, but he had always tried to make me look stupid so many times. I had always wanted to be able to one day stand up to him. It seemed that it was only possible in my dreams. Over and over I would dream of having the opportunity to stand up to him, but I wasn't sure if it was a dream so I was afraid and wouldn't. Then I would wake up and get so mad at myself for not realizing it was just a dream and that I could have gotten away with it in my dream at least to see how it felt.

One day I finally got up the courage to try and make my step dad look stupid. I bought a fake mouse that really looked real. I placed it under the kitchen table. After we ate dinner, I put my acting skills to work. I started screaming because I saw the mouse. Gene went to get a broom and started beating the mouse over and over and over again. After he picked it up to put it in the garbage, he then realized it wasn't real. I was kind of nervous about whether I would get beat for it. He wasn't laughing but I sure was… inside of course. He threw the fake mouse in the garbage and we never heard a word. I was afraid I'd get in trouble but I didn't. It felt so good to finally make him look stupid after all the times he had humiliated us.

Shooting up the Door

After my mothers second time around marrying Gene, she made sure she wasn't home anymore when he got back from being out all night. She would go stay at my grandma's house, my mother's mother. She would leave my brothers and me at home. One morning, I got up for school and my mother was at my grandma's house and the boys were still sleeping. I heard the front door open and it was Gene drunk out of his mind. He started ranting and raving, "Keep laughing behind my back and I'll crack you one."

I was having a glass of milk and a donut at the kitchen table. As I got up from the table to go finish getting ready for school, he knocked the glass of milk out of my hand and punched me in the mouth. I was so shocked! He proceeded by pulling all of the phones out of the wall. Somehow I was able to get to my room and throw some clothes on and get out of there. I ran to my grandma's house and they called the police. He was locked up but not for long.

I was so tired of living in constant violence and fear. I called my father and told him how Gene had given me a fat lip and what had happened. He was furious. He called back later on that night and said he wanted to talk to Gene. I said it's late, the kids are sleeping, and Genes in the bathtub. Let's just forget about everything. My dad said he was coming over, and said "I'm going to kill him." Well, I've heard of that expression many times from people and my father was always a calm person. By the sound of his voice, it sounded like he had been drinking. I didn't believe he meant it. From past experience with my stepfather drinking, he would sometimes pass out. Wishful thinking on my part was that my dad would do the same. Since I never saw a violent side of my father, I really didn't believe he had one. My mother and stepfather were in the next room watching TV. I didn't tell them about the phone call. I went back to bed. Forty-five minutes later the doorbell rang. I was wondering if I should get it, Gene got up to get it. All of a sudden I heard boom boom boom boom boom boom, wood flew everywhere! Someone shot through the door. Bullets went into every room! It was a miracle no one was shot. Ten minutes later the phone rang. I picked it up and my father said, "What's going on?" as he laughed. He didn't do it, but sent someone else to do it. Well, after that the police came and asked me for a picture of my father. I hated to have to give it to them.

The police were out looking for him, but my dad realized that he shouldn't have done it and turned himself in. Actually he had sent someone else to shoot through the door, so he was behind the plan.

I'll never forget how a bullet went through every single piece of clothing hanging on the closet door rack adjacent to the front door.

My jacket was one of those pieces and my mother made me wear it to school everyday with the bullet hole through the front and back.

My stepfather said my father and I had him setup to be killed. So he said I was no longer allowed to answer the phone or the door. He also said I was not allowed to see my father anymore.

Well, I told my mother, "I will see my father, I don't care what Gene says."

She said, "Just lie and say you're going out with your boyfriend." So I did. Since my stepfather was an alcoholic, his driving privileges were taken away and he had to take a bus to work. He would use me as a human shield by making me walk with him every day to the bus stop. He would make me stand there with him until the bus came. He felt he was less apt to get shot at if I were standing next to him.

The Terrible Tragedy

When Sunday came around I said I was going out with my boyfriend, but really I was meeting my father at my grandma's house. We went out for dinner together. His court date was the following day so he was a little nervous and we stayed out a little later than planned.

My grandmother wasn't there this particular time but many other times she had been. There were several times my grandma had opportunities that she took advantage of. She shared the love of the Lord with my dad and always prayed for all of us realizing the seriousness of leaving this world without Jesus

Christ. She made it clear that there was a heaven to gain and a hell to shun. I remember hearing her praying in her room many times crying out for God to have mercy on us, and for all of the family.

When my dad brought me back to my grandma's house, he decided to come in and visit for awhile as he oftentimes did. My stepfather had gotten suspicious since it was late and I hadn't returned home yet, so my mother told him I was with my father.

My dad and I were in the front room of my grand parent's house. My father and I were sitting on the couch talking and my grandpa was there. Then my grandpa stepped out of the house to look for his daughter. My father and I were the only ones remaining in the house. I heard someone coming up the stairs, thinking it was my grandpa returning. The front door was unlocked which was common knowledge.

The door flew open, and there stood my stepfather with a shot gun! He said, "Debbie, go home!" I jumped up from the couch and yelled, "No, don't!"

He immediately shot my father, and was less than two feet away. He shot him in the heart, so he died instantly. At first, I just stood there in shock. Then I started screaming and running down the stairs. I ran to the corner bar screaming for help. I saw a police officer sitting at the bar but he was off duty and ignored me because he didn't want to be bothered so the lady behind the bar called the police and ambulance for me. I couldn't stop screaming, so I was sedated and hospitalized. It's a miracle that I wasn't killed also, considering I was the eye witness to my father's murder. I was in the hospital for several days and was no longer able to speak. The doctors didn't think I would be able to speak again because of the trauma. But they were wrong. Glory to God!

Thank God for the power in a grandma's prayer! I was still very much traumatized and had just started to be able to talk again. Then my mother told me it was my fault that my father was killed, when it could have been prevented if she had telephoned us to warn us ahead of time.

She had told me how she thought of calling but was afraid that if Gene changed his mind, that he might come back and see her on the phone and that he might have killed her. She said if I hadn't told my father about Gene punching me in the mouth, this would have never happened. Then she said, "But I know you didn't know."

It was so hard for me to understand how a mother would not want to be protective of her own child. And I was really tired of having to accept it. It just caused more hurts and bitterness on top of everything else. The story was on the radio and in the newspapers. I went back to school a few weeks later, but no one would talk to me. I guess they didn't know what to say. But it was hard because the family was told not to ever talk about it to me either. The family seemed to think I was handling it well. I was in my third year of high school.

I had returned to school three weeks after the tragedy, but it always seemed so fresh in my mind like it happened yesterday. It was very hard. I would have flashbacks when I would see a father walking with his little girl. I couldn't focus at all on school work. If I heard or saw shooting on TV, I would flashback to the incident. If my friends asked me to go out bowling or something, I would say no. I couldn't because I felt it wouldn't be right to go have a good time, I didn't deserve it. The thoughts of guilt would always be there, "How can you go have fun? You should feel terrible. You should feel bad all the time."

At school, I was offered drugs left and right. I accepted graciously, at least they would help me temporarily forget. I thought I was smart at first, because I was careful as to how much I did and what I took with what. Then I started to just not care anymore. It was a miracle I didn't overdose.

My counselor advised me to quit high school in my third year and I did. I believe that God used him to prevent me from overdosing. My stepfather went to jail and my mother divorced him while he was in jail. When I went to my fathers wake, I saw his friends, I felt like I was walking into an old gangster movie. They were dressed in the typical attire. But they were very kind and sincere.

They told me to call them when Gene got out of prison and that they would take care of him. It felt so nice to finally have power over Gene's life. It was very tempting to accept their offer but I really had so much hate and bitterness that I thought about how nice it would be if I could kill him myself. I thought about the personal satisfaction that I would get out of it. Gene was in prison for less than three years. He didn't have money for an attorney so he had a public defender but still got out early on good behavior.

He pleaded involuntary manslaughter and since he was in for such a short time, I thought, I'm young; if I got arrested; I could do time and then come out after a few years also.

As Gene was in prison I continued to think about the day he would come out. I was wondering if I'd be notified and was surprised that I wasn't. The last time I saw him I was in the courtroom testifying against him. I remember him glaring at me like I was next on his list of things to do.

If I had been notified the day Gene was released from prison, I'm sure I would have called my father's friends to take care of him. It must have been God that intervened. As time went on I thought of how it would affect my brothers if their father was killed. I knew how it affected me when my father was killed. I cared about my two brothers like they were my two sons, since I took care of them so much. They had been through so much, and though their father had done such evil, he was still their father. It might sound crazy but that's what I thought.

It was probably God trying to keep me from going through with my desire to kill him. Anyway, I didn't know where Gene was when he got out. He moved somewhere out of state to hide. I didn't know that until later. I always wondered if I would run in to him one day, if he would come into a restaurant I worked at, etc. and what would happen and how could or would I handle it? I thought of different ways I could kill him and had morbid nightmares on a regular basis.

My mother always told me, before I was even school age, whatever you do Debbie, when you grow up, don't get married!
I listened… I got married before I grew up.

I would feel guilty for the nightmares and wondered if they would ever stop. I felt I had no future. I felt I had no control over my future. Everything seemed so hopeless. Since my mother married my stepfather for the second time around believing he had changed for the better and was definitely wrong, her faith in men was lost.

My mother always told me, before I was even school age, whatever you do Debbie, when you grow up, don't get married!

I was always reminded of these words through out the years. As strange as it sounds, whenever I would watch TV and see the happy couple riding off into the sunset living happily ever after, I pictured and believed that would be me one day, in spite of my mother's unhappiness. She said, "When you grow up, don't get married."

I listened… I got married before I grew up.

Thoughts of fear and constant reminders of how other relatives in the family were unhappy and divorced would come against my mind, but I still believed it would be different for me. It was pretty amazing that in spite of the negative environment that I was raised in that I felt there was hope for me. Thank God for my grandma's prayers!

Trapped and Controlled by Fear

It made me so upset to see my mother feel completely trapped and controlled by fear. I had decided that I would learn from her mistakes. I had made a vow that no man was going to walk on me or control me. I decided that I wasn't going to get married until I was at least twenty five, and that I was going to enjoy my life while it lasted. But at the age of sixteen, someone moved in across the street from me and changed my mind. I'll never forget that day my mother and I viewed the apartment on the third floor. There was a huge Christmas tree standing in the middle of the front room in mid July. Also, the walls had mouse holes in them just like the kind you'd see in cartoons. It was obvious that the prior tenants were feeding them. You could see the morsels of dry dog food they had left in front of each hole. It was scary, but the price was right and the landlord filled the holes. After we moved in, I couldn't help but notice a new neighbor moving in across the street. He was tall, thin, and handsome. I was hoping he would notice me as I was playing paddle ball outside.

He happened to lock his keys in his car one day and came over to introduce himself. I was only sixteen; he was a little older, which I liked because boys my age were very immature.

The summer nights were never long enough as we would sit on his porch and talk until late. I was so happy that Kirk and I had become friends. Every morning I would wake him bright and early to get a ride to school. I still continued to see other people and so did he. One day I was at home and there was a knock at the front door, I was doing the dishes and my little brother answered the door and let the person in, someone I had met at a party a month prior. He knew where I lived because he had walked me home that night. I was surprised when I saw who it was and very nervous because the word on the street was that he had raped a twelve year old girl.

My brother ran downstairs to play with a friend so we were alone. The last thing I wanted to do was be with him, especially alone. I tried to not act nervous afraid that it might set him off. He said a few words and then immediately started attacking me. He only got as far as ripping my clothes, I was able to fight him off and I ran down the stairs as he was chasing after me down the stairs. I ran across the street to Kirk's house. I frantically rang his bell and thank God he was there.

I explained what happened and he called the police. Immediately, three squad cars pulled up on the sidewalk out in front of the apartment. I told them the name of the person and they knew immediately who he was. They said they've picked him up before for indecent exposure, etc. They began searching the area with no success of finding him but said they would definitely be on the look out.

As two of the squad cars were leaving my mother came walking around the corner. "What's going on?" she asked.

I told her what happened. She said she was glad I was alright. I was pretty shaken up and my mom and I started walking up the stairs to our third floor apartment. When she unlocked the door we started to walk in, but screamed because we saw her bedroom door open and saw something moving underneath her sheets.

Thank God that the one of the police officers was still downstairs and heard the scream and came running up the stairs. The Psycho guy had run into our backyard and climbed back into our apartment through our bathroom window and was waiting for me in my mother's bed, naked with a pair of shears. Thank God that nothing happened and that the police caught him.

Several months went by, and Kirk and I decided we no longer wanted to see other people. I guess you could say our friendship had blossomed.

I remember walking in the rain and laughing together. Laughter was what I needed.

At seventeen, three months shy of eighteen, we were married. I am so thankful for my grandma that prayed for me and so thankful that God brought this special man into my life. It was like he was special ordered just for me, God knew what I needed. He was affectionate and loving, and that's what I needed. I felt like I had a reason to live now that I had him, he was definitely God sent. We had an exceptionally good marriage but I also had a lot of baggage that I brought along with me that were filled with hurts and bitterness.

Baggage of Hurt and Bitterness

I guess you could say I had some real issues. Lots of baggage: hurts, bitterness, fear, anger, hatred, vengeance, and low self esteem to mention a few. I used to feel so bad when I would see that Kirk could fall asleep at the drop of a hat, because I couldn't fall asleep. After Kirk fell asleep I would quietly climb out of bed and go in another room. I'd cry myself to sleep hoping he wouldn't hear me, because I didn't want him to feel bad, I also felt it would show a sign of weakness. I was taught to be tough. I would have to smoke marijuana every night to go to sleep. I still had flashbacks when I would hear or see shooting on TV, I would have to go into another room to get away from it. I knew I needed help but didn't believe it was possible to get help.

I knew nothing could undo what had been done. I found it very hard to trust people. There were so many other things that happened that I haven't mentioned. I had a lot of close calls. I didn't see it then, but I know now that God's hand of protection was on me.

It was hard though, and I was so tired and wished there was more to life, but believed it was too good to be true. One of the turning points in my life was when I noticed a change in my cousin. She was married to an alcoholic and she was very unhappy. She was nervous all the time, etc. But all of a sudden I noticed a change in her. She had a calmness that she didn't have before and a sparkle in her eye. It perked my curiosity. I heard she had received Christ into her life but I wasn't really sure about the whole thing.

Some time went by. I also heard that my mother was sick, dying of cancer of the lymph glands. All her joints had visible knots where she was attacked by this disease. Our relationship was not very good, so I felt bad that she was dying especially with bad feelings between us.

I heard that there was nothing the doctors could do for my mother. It was a very rare type of cancer which they had no treatment for. The doctors said that all they could do was observe her.

Eight doctors from Stanford University were on her case because of the fact that it was such a rare type of disease. They said she only has a few weeks to live. She was in the hospital and had gotten down to skin and bones. They said her stomach lining was completely destroyed and there were clusters of ulcers. My cousin that I had seen the change in would say my mom is going to live. I was confused, because, I would ask, "Is that what the doctors said?"

She would say no, and I would get very upset with her. I was glad she was happy now but I thought she had gone off the deep end, if you know what I mean. My grandma, cousin and other people were praying for my mother. My cousin would say, she will live and not die in Jesus name. The name of Jesus is greater than the name of cancer. I didn't understand it. I didn't even pray because I was at a point in my life where I was convinced there was no God. I had thought that God was to blame for all the bad things I had seen and went through in my life and it made me picture God as being cruel.

Since I didn't want to picture God as being cruel I convinced myself that there must not be a God. Of course, I was influenced by the drugs and the evil spirits which had it out for me. The doctors sent tests for the second time and this time said she might have a few months to live. That was better than a few weeks anyway. People in the family that believed kept praying, and saying the name of Jesus is greater than the name of cancer. I would get upset because they would speak positive though the doctors spoke negative.

I couldn't understand. I felt like my cousin was just trying to aggravate me. I said if my mother pulls through this then I'll know that there's a God. The third time tests were sent back to Stanford University, the doctors said, "we don't understand it but her stomach lining is completely restored, the ulcers are completely gone and there's not a trace of cancer in her body!" I was shocked, I did not expect this! The doctors were amazed and I cried for doubting God. After this, it got me to thinking.

But as time went on, I tended to forget as so many of us can and continued living my life as I had. I really wanted to be a better person, mother, and wife. I knew that being depressed was hindering me. I had such bitterness.

Acts 8:23 says "We are poisoned by bitterness."

Darkness

It was eating me up inside. I grew up in such darkness that I never took the time to look up at the sky when I walked outside. I never even thought about it. When I saw someone on TV lying under a tree admiring the sky, I thought, *how silly, what a waste of time, oh, that's just TV.* All I could think about was putting one foot in front of the other to get to where I was going. As I grew older and even when I married, I would rely on a drink or drinks to relax me or numb me, or to have confidence, when it really was a counterfeit for what God had to offer through a relationship with Jesus Christ. As I started to study the Bible I found a Scripture that said not to be drunk with wine but to be filled with the spirit. Ephesians 5:8. It made me think about how, more so long ago, but how still from time to time you see signs at bars that read wine and spirits, a thought to ponder.

The void inside that I once tried to fill with other things finally was filled by receiving Jesus Christ, and by drawing closer to him. I received what I really needed: righteousness, peace and joy.

"For the kingdom of God is not a matter of eating and drinking, but of righteousness, peace, and joy in the Holy Spirit." Romans 14:17

Now instead of reaching for a drink, I drink of the spirit of God and have a deeper and more satisfying experience.

Instead of relying on a drink, I rely on God to be my confidence, my comforter, and my friend through reading the Bible and praying. When I read his Word, I feel peace and joy increase in my life, like a supernatural high.

All I'm trying to tell you is that, "There's nothing like the real thing." Nothing can compare to Jesus.

As Jesus was praising the Father, the Lord of Heaven and earth, it states that Jesus was "full of joy through the Holy Spirit." Luke 10:31

We also can experience this same joy through the Holy Spirit as we praise him. It is possible to live in a higher realm through the spirit of Jesus Christ. When I found out that God's word says that he is our confidence, I started to thank God. I said, "Thank you God that you are my confidence," it really started changing the way I felt. Each day as I would pray, I would thank him again. I became more and more free.

"In the fear of the Lord is strong confidence: and his children shall have a place of refuge." Proverbs 14:26

I'm so thankful that I'm free from fear, that I'm free to be me, without having to have a drink to be my crutch.

I used to try to fill the void inside of me just as so many people do with things. My spirit was so empty, my mind was so depressed; neither alcohol, drugs, nor anything else was able to fill that void inside.

Prince of Peace

Then I heard that Jesus Christ was the Prince of peace, and that he was the healer of the broken hearted. He is our peace that has broken down every wall. It is only his love that can drive away our fears, heal our hearts and satisfy the longing in our souls. I've been there where life is hard and it makes it even harder when you think that God makes the bad happen. When I thought about all the things I had been through and had seen in my life, it made me picture God as being cruel. I didn't want to picture God as being cruel so I convinced myself that there must not be a God, after all.

This was the truth that I knew, and the truth that I knew was really a lie that hurt a lot. My mother would often tell me how she wished she never had children. One might think it was at a moment of anger and that she really didn't mean it, but it wasn't the case. Just out of the blue, her mouth would open and out came the words. I would just listen to the words and feel hurt, not knowing what to say.

Two years after we were married I became happily pregnant with our first child. I was so excited to share the news.

I expected my mother to rejoice with me, especially since she knew I had a good husband that would be a good father to our children. But instead of being happy for me, she was jealous. As twisted as that sounds, it was the case. Instead of saying I'm so happy for you that you found someone that's a good husband and father, she would say the opposite. She would snarl at me and say, "You're happy. You have a good husband. I never did."

As if it wasn't fair that I did and that I should feel bad about it. I would say." I don't understand why you wouldn't be happy for me."

"I wish I never had children, how could you want to have children? I don't understand how anyone would want to have children," she said.

Finally one day I spoke up when she reminded me once again about how she felt. I said, "Thanks a lot; it's like a slap in my face. I've always been respectful to you, why would you say that when you know it hurts me."

She would reply by saying, "Well, it's true."

Her words had nothing to do with there being a behavior problem. Sure my brothers had their moments, but I remember the joys they brought into our life also. My brothers were very good, considering the bad home environment that they had come from. And no, I wasn't perfect but I was taught to respect my mother. Though I did not feel respect for her, I treated her with respect anyway. It was very hard to do though when she constantly said hurtful things and was not there to protect me.

The Greatest Day of my Life

I'll never forget the night I asked Jesus Christ to come into my heart and life. I had been married for three years and though our financial struggles were a strain on our marriage, we loved each other very much. I was so happy to have our two year old daughter that I had always desired to have, but my husband and daughter could not fill the void within my heart. And only Jesus could heal the hurts from my past. It was late one evening after my husband and daughter had fallen asleep. I was alone in my front room and I heard someone on the television say that Jesus loves you and will heal your hurts. He said I could pray a prayer right where I was. So I did, I asked Jesus to forgive me of my sins and to come into my heart.

I felt such heaviness and darkness leave me. I felt so different that I actually went into the bathroom to look in the mirror to see if I looked different. That's how different I felt! I remember that night I felt such a peace that I never felt before.

I was finally able to go to sleep at night without having to cry myself to sleep or smoke as I did so many nights before. It wasn't too good to be true!

"I cried to the Lord and he heard me. I lay down and slept, I awoke and the Lord sustained me." Psalm 3: 4-5. Ephesians 2:14 states, "Jesus himself is our peace." Psalm 127:2 explains, "He gives his beloved sleep."

I finally found the truth and it set me free from depression. As I searched the Scriptures, I found out that depression is actually a spirit.

The Bible says in Isaiah 61:3 "Put on the garment of praise for the spirit of heaviness" which is depression.

God's word is full of power; it worked then, and still works.

It is powerful when we hear it, meditate on it, speak it and act on it.

We must remember it is not mind over matter, not positive thinking but God's word that has spiritual power.

The word of faith must be in your mouth and your heart to work effectively.

"The word is nigh thee, even in thy mouth, and in thy heart: that is the word of faith, which we preach." Romans 10:8-10

"The grass withers, the flower fades, but the word of our God stands forever." Isaiah 40:8

As I continued to read the Bible, I Realized that my mother was without Christ, and therefore she was under a curse. To my surprise, I came across a Scripture in the book of Deuteronomy. It said one of the curses from a long list of curses was that you will have children and not enjoy them. Up until then it was hard for me to understand how any mother could ever feel that way. It made me feel better when I discovered the Scripture in the book of Galatians 3:13 NKJV: It says that "Jesus Christ redeemed us from the curse." I was so thankful I had received

Christ into my life and that he redeemed me from the curse and so I could have children and enjoy them.

Words cannot express the joy that they have brought to my heart and continue to bring. I started going to a church that taught the Bible and how it was like a love letter to us from God. That really made it more enjoyable to find that it was really written to each of us personally. It was so nice to know that God was good.

"Taste and see that the Lord is good; blessed are they that take refuge in him." Psalm 34:8 NIV

It was so wonderful to know that God didn't make the bad happen but would help me through the bad and that things were subject to change.

I had a lot of hurts from my mother not being there for me in my life. It was hard to understand why she wouldn't want to protect me like a mother normally would.

But God started helping me to understand that she wasn't normal. And that all the hurtful things that she would say and all the lies that she told others about me, were words planned by the enemy to destroy me.

God reminded me of how we need to know who our enemy is. Just as God will bring people into our lives to bless us, the devil will use people in our life to try and destroy us. The enemy knew that by using my mother he would be more effective in hurting me, and it was hard but it helped me when I found out who my enemy really was. The devil wanted me to just think it was just my mother being so mean to me and by the way she treated me that she couldn't possibly love me so I would continue to feel hurt.

As I started understanding the Scripture, it became clear that it was an evil spirit working against me through her. If I listened to the thoughts that came into my head I had difficulty, because the devil would bring thoughts to my mind saying, no it's your mother, she's just mean. The Bible made it very clear that it is more than people but people that are influenced by evil spirits. "We do not fight against flesh and blood but against principalities, against powers, against the rulers of the darkness of this world, against spiritual wickedness in high places." Ephesians 6:12

It was also so nice to know that things were subject to change by praying, reading the word and applying it to my life.

A New Perspective

As I immersed myself in God's word and prayed, God helped me to see things differently concerning my mother. As I set my will to do his will, God helped me. He helped me to think about how she had been through a lot in her life. He continually reminded me of the Scripture that "we do not fight against flesh and blood but against principalities, against powers, against the rulers of the darkness of this world, against spiritual wickedness in high places." Ephesians 6:12

I was also reminded of the Scripture how we've been given power over all the power of the enemy and how we need to not be conformed to this world but be transformed by the renewing of our minds with God's word. We need to cast down the evil thoughts and replace them with the truth of God's word. The Lord helped me to love and forgive her in spite of the hurt I felt. The Lord helped me by meditating on Scriptures from the Bible about love. How God is love and how his love is shed abroad in our heart by the Holy Spirit. As we abide in him we have the ability to love as he loves and his love never fails.

As I continued on my new spiritual journey, it was so wonderful to know that my relationship with Christ was changing everything. I knew that religion wasn't the answer. I had tried that in my past, as a child. I saw how different religions had their certain rules and beliefs and how a lot of them believed some of the Bible but not all of it. I believe that religions were the result of man's ego. I was tired of religion. I wanted to know what God had to say, not what some religion that someone made up had to say. As I read the Bible I found that God didn't say, "If anyone is in a certain religion they become new."

I found that the Bible made it clear that I needed a relationship with God, not a religion Just as it says in 2 Corinthians 5:17, "If anyone is in Christ they become a new creation; old things pass away and all things become new." As I started spending time in the word and in prayer, I felt closer to God. As I learned to praise and worship him, I experienced his divine presence. I found that in his presence was where I started being changed.

The more I was in the Lord's presence, the more joy I received, the more peace I experienced and the more God's love flowed to and through me. I started looking forward to each day with an excitement and expectancy in my heart which resulted in living in a higher realm of life.

This is the exciting life you can live as well. Whatever pain or bitterness that you are carrying, I encourage you to give it to the Lord. I ask of you to accept Jesus Christ as your personal Savior and experience his divine forgiveness so you can also live in a higher realm of life.

CHAPTER 3

The Harmful Effects of Unforgiveness

Even modern medicine and psychiatry have shown us that holding unforgiveness can put your health in danger. Unforgiveness may be directed at someone else or by not forgiving yourself. It is always accompanied by anger and resentment and is a leading cause of many physical ailments, including hypertension, ulcerative colitis, and toxic goiters.

Research has shown that people who are deeply and unjustly hurt by others can heal emotionally, and in some cases physically by forgiving their offender. Better Health Research shows that resentment and a general lack of forgiveness raises blood pressure, depletes immune systems, makes you more easily depressed causing enormous stress to the body. It also causes people to hold weight.

According to studies, Doctors have found that there is a huge relationship between forgiveness and health. The fact is after being hurt, angry, suffering loss, real or false guilt, or envy, the blocked love flow profoundly affects the way your body functions, thus your health. This can cause alterations in the pattern of chemicals and electricity in your body. It also disrupts the harmony of the brain waves, making you less able to think clearly and to make good decisions.

Stress of not having a Forgiving Spirit

Unforgiveness distresses your muscular-skeletal system by increasing forehead muscle tension, thereby producing headaches, and by also producing other symptoms: stomach aches, muscle tension, joint pain/aches, dizziness and tiredness. For example, your muscles may tighten, causing imbalances or pain in your neck, back and limbs. There is decreased blood flow to the joint surfaces. This makes it more difficult for the blood to remove wastes from the tissues. It reduces the supply of oxygen and nutrients to the cells. This increases chances of delayed or inadequate repair during sleep, impairing recovery from injury, arthritis, etc. It can cause your teeth to clench at night contributing to problems with your teeth and jaw joints. Injury through inattention, accident, or violence is more likely.

The peptide and hormonal chemical "messengers" are altered in every system of the body. The

blood flow to your heart is constricted. Your digestion is impaired.

Your breathing is restricted. Since your immune
system doesn't function as well, you become more
vulnerable to infections, and perhaps malignancy.
You feel bad, and your mind is less able to see its
way through difficulties. The list goes on. Indeed
it becomes a list of many of the diseases seen by
doctors all over the world.

And while forgiveness may not be the sole
cause of all of them, it increases your vulnerability
to them. It can set the scene for them, and it can
delay or even prevent your recovery. The effects
when you are unforgiving to yourself can include
depression; low self esteem; depriving yourself of
the good opportunities that life offers you; punishing yourself through activities or relationships that
work out to harm yourself; addictions and so on.

The alternative to forgiveness is bitterness and
resentment. People who refuse to forgive hurt themselves. Bitter people are no fun to be around. They
can't sleep. Ulcers line their stomach. They see
the negative in every situation because their life is
filled with these feelings of resentment and anger.
People who are unwilling to forgive may feel they
are punishing the other person but the only person
paying the price is themselves.

According to the Bible if you harbor bitter envy
and contention/selfish ambition in your hearts,
you will find disorder and every evil practice.
This wisdom does not come down from above but

is earthly, unspiritual, and even demonic. James 3:14-16

As I traveled through life I started to realize that if the enemy can't get us to walk away from God, he will try the next best thing by getting us to not forgive, because it hinders our prayers and therefore affects our relationship with God.

David the Psalmist wrote, "If I regard iniquity in my heart the Lord will not hear." Psalm 66:18 If God doesn't hear our prayers, our prayers are hindered. If God doesn't hear when we pray we pray without power.

God commands us to walk in love.

"Jesus said a new commandment I give unto you, that you love one another, as I have loved you, that you also love one another." John 13:34

I'm so thankful that God didn't say to forgive just to make things difficult for us. Just as an earthly father will tell us to listen for our own good, God tells us for our own good because when we walk in love, we are under God's protection. When we walk out of love, we walk out from under God's protection. "Let all bitterness, and wrath, and anger, and clamor, and evil speaking, be put away from you, with all malice. And be kind one to another, tenderhearted, forgiving one another, even as God for Christ's sake has forgiven you." Ephesians 4:31-32

Benefits of Forgiving
The benefits of forgiving are recently being discovered by science and have long been taught

by religious organizations. Scientifically validated benefits of forgiving include the reduction of chronic pain, cardiovascular problems, a reduction of violent behavior, increased hope, and decreased levels of depression and anxiety.

Burden Lifted

Most people, however, when they have reached forgiveness describe having a change in feelings, behaviors, and thoughts. They feel a huge burden lifted from their shoulders and think much more clearly. They are filled with compassion and love for the offender. They also have no more desire to pursue justice regarding the offender. Their thoughts and actions no longer focus on revenge. In order for forgiveness to take place, a softening of the heart needs to occur in the heart of the offended. Many people have found prayer to be an invaluable part of the forgiveness process. Inviting divine help as you try to forgive someone who has offended you is a powerful way to experience a change of heart. Forgiveness is God's antidote for anger.

Maybe you feel that you can't forgive. I believe that if you know the Creator and choose to be strong in him that you can. Just as God's mercy and grace has a transforming effect in your life, your extension of that grace to others has power to transform them. An act of forgiveness is the result of God working through us enabling us to love as even he loves as we abide in him. It's not natural but is supernatural, that's why so many say, "How can I forgive? I can't forgive."

Forgiveness is not an emotion but is an act of the will, as we set our will to do God's will. God will honor our obedience and will fill us with his love and power. As you pray for your offender you will begin to feel the compassion and love that the Lord has for them and you will experience a release and a freedom as a result.

Dr. Enright and Zell 1989 believe that forgiveness should include both love and letting go of anger in spite of unjust injury. Misunderstanding still abounds regarding the true meaning of forgiveness. Often, people say, "Forgive and forget"

But how can we forget the horrible things we have endured? How can we forget the wounds and scars we wear each day? How can we forget the Holocaust? We need to forgive and remember, so that the evil will not be repeated. Others say, "Forgiveness means that we need to excuse, condone, or pardon the wrongs done to us."

But wrong is still wrong, regardless of whether we forgive the offender.

When one forgives, one does not open a jail cell door but has an effective and possibly behavioral transformation toward the injurer; one can forgive and see justice realized. Some equate forgiveness with reconciliation, but how can we invite the perpetrators back into our lives, when there is no apology and no willingness to change their destructive ways?

True Forgiveness

Forgiveness is not intended to turn us into willing victims! Ideally, the forgiveness process may lead to reconciliation, but it has to be a reciprocal relationship, and involves acknowledging wrong — doing and making amends. Unilateral forgiveness does not necessarily lead to reconciliation. We need to know the difference between forgiveness and reconciliation. It is also important to differentiate between pseudo forgiveness and genuine forgiveness. When we say we have forgiven someone, but still harbor grudges and resentments or maintain an attitude of indifference and neutrality, we have only achieved pseudo forgiveness. Complete forgiveness involves complete transformation toward the offender.

To some, it seems reasonable to maintain a psychological or physical difference to avoid getting hurt again, until there is some indication that the perpetrator has changed his or her ways, but others would argue that such psychological barriers should disappear when one has completed the forgiveness process.

Again, Enright and Zell write, "Forgiveness is more than a moral imperative, more than a theological dictum. It is the only means, given our humanness and imperfections, to overcome hate and condemnation and proceed with the business of growing and loving."

We may not be able to forgive on our own but there is a power greater than any other. This is a song the Lord inspired me to write after he helped me to forgive someone that I could never have forgiven on my own.

There is a power
There is a power greater than any other
It comes from above, it is the Fathers love
There is a power greater than any other
It comes from above it is the Fathers love
Human love, it will end, but Jesus love it will mend
broken hearts, broken lives of any kind.
And it's love to love the people you couldn't love before
Love to conquer anger that comes knockin knockin knockin at your door.
This love will win you over no matter what life brings
And this love it comes from him, it only comes from him
Just reach your hand to Jesus; he's reaching out to you
And by the power of God's word your mind will be renewed.
This is the power that's greater than any other, it comes from above it is the Father's love.

Maybe no one murdered or abused or tormented you or your family. Maybe someone hurt you as a child, or hurt your child, maybe your spouse cheated on you. For some it could be a lot of little offenses that kept adding up over the years that have accumulated into bitterness. We may not be able to stop some of the pains in life from happening but we can stop punishing ourselves and leave it up to God. "Just and true are his ways." Revelation 16:3

"Don't say I will recompense evil. Wait for the Lord and he will deliver you." Proverbs 20:22

"Don't overcome by evil, but overcome evil with good." Romans 12:21 NIV

"Get rid of all bitterness, rage, and anger, brawling and slander, along with every form of malice. Be kind and compassionate to one another, forgiving each other, just as in Christ God forgave you." Ephesians 4:31-32 NIV

Above all things have intense and unfailing love for one another, for love covers a multitude of sins forgives and disregards the offenses of others. 1 Peter 4:8 Amplified

Forgiving Those Who Have Wronged You A Lot

You may say, "I will forgive those who have wronged me a little, but not the ones that wronged me a lot." I remember how I went down my list of people and how I felt that way at first, but then I found that I needed help from above, God's love. If you desire God's blessings, you must forgive.

"If you forgive people their sins, your Father in Heaven will forgive your sins also. If you do not forgive people their sins, your father will not forgive your sins." Matthew 6:14-15 NLV

"You may say it's not possible, but with God it is possible." Matthew 19:26 NIV

"We can do all things through Christ who strengthens us." Philippians 4:13

Whoever claims to live in him must walk as Jesus did. 1 John 2:6 NIV

"A heart of peace gives life to the body, but envy rots the bones." Proverbs 14:30

"Kingdom living is righteousness, peace, and joy in the Holy Spirit." Romans 14:17

"My peace I'll give to you, not as the world gives, a peace that passes all understanding." John 14:27

"He heals the brokenhearted." Psalm 147:3

"The Lord is near to all that call upon him sincerely and in truth." Psalm 145:18

"Come to me, all you who are heavy laden, and I will give you rest, Take my yoke upon you and learn from me, for I am gentle and you will find rest for your soul." Matthew 11:28-29

"I cried to the Lord and he heard me. I lay down and slept, I awoke and the Lord sustained me." Psalm 3:4-5

As I read Psalm 91, it helped me to understand how God's promises are conditional.

It explains how as we dwell in that secret place of the most high, we abide under the shadow of the almighty, how he covers you and protects you.

God is love, so when we walk out of love, we are not under the shadow of the Almighty any longer. We walk out from under his protection.

When we are in unforgiveness, we walk out of love.

Psalm 91 is one of my favorite Psalms, whenever I think of it I can't help but be reminded of God's great love for us and how he restored my memory.

God is a restorer

There was a time in my life that my memory had been affected very badly. I would invite my mother and her new husband over for dinner and I wouldn't be home when they arrived because I would forget that I had invited them. My memory was so bad that I would forget I left the stove burner on and leave the house.

When I received the Lord, I found the Scripture, "The memory of the righteous is blessed." Proverbs 10:7

I cried out to the Lord and asked him to restore my memory, not only did he restore my memory but he even helped me during that time to memorize Psalm 91:1-16 Amplified

Those who live in the shelter of the Most High will find rest in the shadow of the Almighty. This I declare about the LORD: He alone is my refuge, my place of safety; he is my God, and I trust him. For he will rescue you from every trap and protect you from deadly disease. He will cover you with his feathers. He will shelter you with his wings. His faithful promises are your armor and protection. Do not be afraid of the terrors of the night, nor the arrow that flies in the day. Do not dread the disease that stalks in darkness, nor the disaster that strikes at midday. Though a thousand fall at your side, though ten thousand are dying around you, these evils will not touch you. Just open your eyes, and see how the wicked are punished. If you make the LORD your refuge, if you make the Most High your shelter, no evil will conquer you; no plague will come near your home. For he will order his angels to protect you wherever you go. They will hold you up with their hands so you won't even hurt your foot on a stone. You will trample upon lions and cobras; you will crush fierce lions and serpents under your feet! The LORD says, "I will rescue those who love me. I will protect those who trust in my name. When they call on me, I will answer; I will be with them in trouble. I will rescue and honor them. I will reward them with a long life and give them my salvation."

God is a God of restoration. "The memory of the righteous is blessed." Proverbs 10:7

I'm so thankful that God gave me the ability to memorize his Word. His wonderful words gave me the ability to retrain my thinking and to realize his great love for me. Perhaps God is leading you to start to memorize his word. Why don't you start with the first verse of Psalm 91 and then try the next one. You'll be surprised at how much strength keeping God's Words in your heart will give you right now.

CHAPTER 4

God Gives the Desires of Your Heart

A s I first started reading the Bible, one of the first Scriptures that I found was "Delight in the Lord and he will give you the desires of your heart," in Psalm 37:4

I was so surprised that God was really that good. It seemed too good to be true, but I found that it was God's word to us. I became very excited about it. I also found the Scripture that said God watches over his Word to perform it, and that he's not a man that he'd lie. "God is not a man, that he should lie, nor a son of man, that he should change his mind. Does he speak and then not act? Does he promise and not fulfill?" Numbers 23:19 NIV

"In hope of eternal life, which God, cannot lie, promised before the world began." Titus 1:2

Delight in the Lord

As I delighted in the Lord, I found it to be true and I started learning that as we put him first, all these things are added unto us. I was so touched that God loved me that much that he would give me the desires of my heart. It made me think about how my father had always promised to take me to Greece. Since my father's life was taken, he wasn't able to fulfill his promise of taking me to Greece. But my Heavenly Father showed me through his Word that he cared enough. And that he was watching out for me now. I then had an excitement and expectancy in my heart that somehow God would make it possible for me to go to Greece. Because I delighted in him and it was a desire of my heart.

Three weeks later, after opening the door of my heart to Jesus Christ, I heard a knock at the door of my apartment. It was a man from Russia with a letter in his hand. He said it was from my grandparents in Greece. This really happened! He said they had been searching for me, and was about to put it on TV. He read me the letter. He said they want to meet you and will send you two round trip tickets to Greece. They said I don't even have to pack a suitcase with clothes, they'll buy me clothes. I was on cloud nine! This was my first experience of seeing the supernatural power of God move in this way. It was so exciting! I felt so loved! To think there were people I'd never met in my life that loved me. I had always longed to meet them and they were searching for me?! It was very amazing!

When my two year old daughter and I got off the plane in Greece, everyone was at the airport waiting for us. It was amazing how there were all these people I'd never seen before in my life, yet felt so much love from them. It impacted my life in a great way. I was so thankful.

I had always felt bad about the fact that my daughter was never able to meet my father, her grandfather so it was such a blessing that God made it possible for her to meet my father's father, her great grandfather, and great grandmother. It was an awesome experience!

Our stay was cut short since the food didn't agree with my daughter, but it was truly an experience I'll never forget. That was just the beginning of my getting to know my miracle working God. When I returned home I looked forward to continuing my new relationship with my Heavenly Father and was very excited about getting closer to him. My relatives in Greece spoke very little English and I spoke very little Greek so my one cousin that did speak English was the mediator. We communicated mainly by writing letters, and on occasion we would talk by phone.

The Ultimate Sacrifice of our Savior

A few years after our trip to Greece, I gave birth to our son. We were so thankful for a healthy boy, especially since I had a miscarriage a year prior. A few weeks after he was born, I received a phone call from my cousin in Greece. He said my Uncle had a favor to ask of me. I couldn't imagine what he would want from me. He said that my Uncle heard that I had a son and that his wife and he had been unable to have children. They were thinking about adopting but would rather have blood. He wants to know if you would give him your son, since you're young, you can always have more. He explained how well off my Uncle was so he would take good care of our son and give him a good education.

I was so shocked, I started laughing. I said, "Come on, your're joking." He said, "No, he's serious." I still couldn't believe my ears. I had so many mixed emotions. I was shocked, hurt, and upset that they would think I would ever consider such a crazy thing. I tried to take in consideration that when my Uncle was eighteen that he was in the army and a grenade went off in his face that had blinded him. I thought it must have done more than just blinded him but affected his mind as well. They finally did adopt a little girl some years later. I guess when they had the experience of having a child of their own, they realized to ask of me such a favor as giving up my child was not humane so they had my cousin call to apologize to me.

The experience made me realize how God loved us that he gave up his only son and how hard it must have been.

God knew that the price to pay for our sins would be blood, the blood of his one and only Son. He knew Jesus would have to die a terrible death and that only his blood could be the payment for our sins so that we might have eternal life. I'm so thankful that God gave up his only son for us.

In this the love of God was manifested toward us, that God has sent his only begotten son into the world, that we might live through him.

"In this is love, not that we loved God, but that he loved us and sent his son to be the propitiation for our sins." 1 John 4:9-10 NKJV

The cost was the cross, the price has been paid. The blood of Jesus will never lose its power. It speaks healing and forgiveness. "For you were bought at a price." 1 Corinthians 6:20 "We were purchased with the blood of Jesus Christ." Acts 20:28

"For this is my blood of the New Testament, which was shed for many for the remission of sins." Matthew 26:28 NJV

"There was only one that was perfect, Jesus Christ; he came to put away sin by the sacrifice of himself." Hebrews 9:26

"But if we walk in the light, as he is in the light, we have fellowship one with another, and the blood of Jesus Christ his son cleanses us from all sin." 1 John 1:7

"Without shedding of blood there is no remission". Hebrews 9:22 NKJV

What can wash away our sins? Nothing but the blood of Jesus.

The Miracle of the House

As my children grew to be certain ages I would remember how it was to be that age. I remember hearing how often times when we grow up in such dysfunctional homes how we can unfortunately marry into it also. It helped me to not take it for granted and to be truly thankful for having a good husband and a home that was safe for my children and me. I am so thankful for a wonderful husband as well as a wonderful father. He has always been there for all our children, and has always gone beyond the call.

"In reverent and worshipful fear of the Lord there is strong confidence, and his children shall always have a place of refuge." Proverbs 14:26 Amplified

"The living, the living—they shall thank and praise you, as I do this day; the Father shall make known to the children your faithfulness and your truth." Isaiah 38:19 Amplified

One hot summer day, I had put the wading pool outside for my three year old son, Kirk, and his cousin, Jamie, to play in.

We lived in a small apartment. Outside was a small patch of grass in between two blocks of concrete. After they finished playing, I brought the pool inside.

While ironing in the kitchen my son came in. "Mommy, why can't we leave the pool outside?"

I said, "If we do someone might take it."

He asked why his other cousin that lived with his grandma left his swimming pool outside and we couldn't. I explained how they lived in a house with a yard and a fence where it was safe.

He asked, "Why can't we have a house, yard and a fence so we can have a swimming pool outside too?

"Well, I'll have to pray about that."

I didn't really take to heart what he had asked. Minutes later he came back into the kitchen asking, "Well, did you pray?"

I said, "Oh, no!"

So I prayed. "Father, it would be nice if we had a house with a yard and a fence so we could have a swimming pool outside."

After praying Kirk went back to play. Maybe since I grew up living in apartments, I never had a desire for a house. Or maybe because I grew up without and in such a negative environment, I never dreamed of it being possible.

The next day I woke up with the desire and expectancy in my heart of getting a house! I was so surprised because I never had the desire in all my life until after that day of praying that prayer.

When my husband arrived home from work, I said, "Guess what?" "We're getting a house!"

He said, "What are you talking about? We barely make it now to pay our rent each month."

I explained how God put the desire in my heart and the expectancy after the day I prayed. It did look impossible. We had no money saved, and no credit established. I said I know that God put this desire in my heart.

Let's pray to God for wisdom on what we should do. We prayed and were led to sell one of our cars for money as a down payment. One day, my husband picked me up from a restaurant I had worked at. It was a slow day so I had only made eight dollars.

On the way home, we started to pass a realty office, I said, "Let's stop in and tell them we're looking for a house."

He said, "We don't have the money."

"We don't have to tell them that," I said.

They tried to discourage us when we told them the price range we were looking for. They took us to see houses in that price range but ones that had no stairs so it wasn't possible to go in to see the house. Or houses so small they looked like garages. We still believed with God all things were possible. They called us a couple weeks later and said they found the house for us. It was a nice house in the price range we were looking for! The only problem was we needed $2000 more.

My husband had a profit sharing program at work which was not allowed to borrow from. But two weeks after we prayed, it was changed to a 401k program allowing him to borrow the remaining amount we needed to buy the house. We know it was not a coincidence.

After we moved into the house, I remember calling my cousin. "We can get cabinets, which we really need or a huge swimming pool, I said to her, "What do you think I should do?"

"Oh, buy the swimming pool, what kind of memories will cabinets give you?" she said.

A swimming pool it was. God made it possible to buy the house with a huge yard, fence and a nice big new Ester Williams swimming pool- not a wading pool!

It's interesting how after a period of time goes by we can tend to forget some things. Later on, after we had our first house, a friend of mine reminded me of how she remembered that our son, Kirk Douglas, was the one that originally had the desire for the house with a yard and a fence and a swimming pool and he's the one that made sure that I prayed about it. Then I remembered and said, that's right, "He delighted in the Lord and was given the desire of his heart."

It's interesting how God placed the desire in my heart the day after my son asked me to pray about it and as my husband and I prayed and sought God, how He brought it about. God cares about every little thing, from great to small, he cares about them all.

Nothing is too small to God and nothing is too big for God. I hope these stories inspire you to believe and expect because all things are possible to those who believe.

Learning to Hear Gods Voice

As I was driving to work one day, I was feeling a strong desire in my heart to be closer to God. I was talking with the Lord and said, "What can I do to become closer to you? I want to know you more. I want to hear your voice. I want to be led by your spirit."

He said, "Stop eating lunch, and spend time in my word instead."

So I did. As I desired to know him more I started drawing closer to him and he started drawing closer to me. James 4:8

"In the beginning was the word, the word was with God and the word was God," John 1:1

Since the Word is God and I started spending more time in the Word, I became closer to God. I was working at a bakery. When it came time for lunch, I would go downstairs and find a corner to myself and have some juice while reading and meditating in the word.

Each day I continued to have my juice and read God's Word. As time went on, I found that since I was feeding my spirit more than my body my spirit was growing stronger and was becoming more sensitive to the spirit of God, so I became more in tune to hearing his voice. I've seen and heard of people who have fasted but not spent time in the word of God and that's a dangerous thing to do.

The Bible tells us to be careful because there are other voices in the world. In the Bible it warns us that the devil will disguise himself as an angel of light.

"The devil makes himself look like an angel of light." 2 Corinthians 11:14 NLV

God speaks to us through his word, if we are in the word and in prayer, and praying according to God's word we will hear his voice and the voice of a stranger we will not follow. "My sheep hear my voice; I know them and they follow me." John 10:27 NIV

If the voice we hear doesn't agree with the word of God it is not God's voice. God and his word are one and the same. That's why it is very important to be in God's word daily and that's why the devil will try to keep you away from reading God's word. If we are not in the word it is easier for us to be deceived. As I drew closer to God I started experiencing his love and compassion for the lost.

"For Christ's love compels us because we are convinced that one died for all, and therefore all died." 2 Corinthians 5:14 NIV

I started getting a revelation of how we are his hands and feet. How we are here on this earth as his representatives. Though his body has ascended into Heaven we are his body and how his spirit lives within us. He wants to use us and as we make ourselves available to him, his spirit will possess us and he will lead and guide us. God is looking for those whose hearts are towards him.

"The eyes of the Lord run to and fro throughout the whole earth to show himself strong on the behalf of them whose heart is perfect toward him." 2 Chronicles 16:9

A Free Cab Ride

I was getting ready to leave work for the day, and planned on taking a bus, actually two buses to get home as usual. But then I heard a voice say, take a cab home. It wasn't an audible voice that anyone else could hear. I heard it in my spirit. I was really surprised because the words were perfectly clear just as clear as if a person told me the words.

In response, I said, "But a cab will cost more money," Again it was within I responded.

Then I heard a voice say, "Well, I want you to take a cab."

I knew it was God, so I said okay. He said, "Go on now, hurry up." Notice, he said it in a language that I understood, Not, thou shalt quickly leaveth. I'm glad God isn't religious like some people, aren't you?

"A cab will be coming around the corner as soon as you get outside," he said.

Sure enough, as soon as I stepped outside the door, a cab came around the corner. I flagged it down and got in. He asked where I was going and I gave him my address. As we were driving the Lord started telling me about how this man driving the cab really needed to know how much Jesus loved him. So I started sharing with him about how much Jesus loved him, about how Jesus died for him personally and if he was the only one that Jesus would have still died just for him. As I spoke you could feel the presence of the Lord fill the taxicab. It was really awesome. If you can imagine how it feels when someone has shown love to you, well, it was magnified many times more than human love could be. That's the best way I can describe it.

Then the Lord told me he wanted me to sing a song to the cab driver and he gave me the words and melody. I asked the cab driver if it was alright that

I sang a song and he said yes. This is the song that the Lord gave me:

Jesus is a Reality

Jesus is a reality, Jesus is a reality, he's saved me, rearranged me changed my life and changed my heart, he's made me new, why don't you make Jesus a reality?

He will change you supernaturally, oh, greater love has no man, than this laying down his life for his friend, he'll never end.

Jesus is a reality; he was always and forever shall be Jesus a reality

He'll change you, rearrange you, change your life and change your heart, he'll make a new man out of you. Receive Jesus, he's a reality.

Jesus a reality.

It was very interesting; the cab driver seemed very receptive, to say the least. After we arrived to my destination he said he wanted to pray to receive this Jesus Christ. I shared with him about how by confessing with his mouth that Jesus is Lord and by believing in his heart that God raised Jesus from the dead that he would be saved. "With the heart you believe unto righteousness; and with the mouth confession is made onto salvation. Whoever believes on him will not be ashamed."Romans10:9-11

After we prayed I asked how much I owed him and he said nothing. He was so overwhelmed by the love of Christ that he said, "I am a Muslim and nobody has ever talked to me about Jesus like you have." What you've given me could not compare to any amount of money." He knew that he now had a hope in Jesus Christ since he accepted him as his savior. He refused to take any money. Isn't that just like God?

Then to prove his sincerity, he came to church that Sunday with us and he took off his shoes. I didn't know why he took them off at first but it is a Muslim custom, now I know he felt it was being respectful to take your shoes off. "Do not come any closer," God said. "Take off your sandals, for the place where you are standing is holy ground." Exodus 3:5 NIV

Exceeding Love

One day my husband and I were driving to a friends' house where we had been invited over for dinner. On our way there I had told Kirk how it had been so long since I had last bought a new dress. I had shared with him how I had been tempted to use some of the grocery money, but I didn't. "Well," he said, "I'm sorry but we don't have the money right now. Why don't you talk to God about it?" Then I thought about how it was a desire in my heart and how I delight in the Lord, and how the Scripture in Psalm 37:4 says, "Delight in the Lord, and he'll give you the desires of your heart."

When we arrived at their house, they had a wonderful chicken dinner waiting for us. We had a really nice visit. I went into their bathroom and I was admiring the color scheme. It was such a pretty turquoise and tan combination. I hadn't said anything to anyone about it. I just thought about it within. I didn't tell Kirk or anyone. Though God knows our heart, I didn't realize he was paying attention.

Two weeks later, we had the same friends over for dinner that had invited us over.

When they walked in the door, my friend Diane was carrying a huge box. "What's that, I asked?"

"It's something that God told me to buy for you and he said to tell you he loves you," she said.

I was so surprised that I didn't know what to say. "Open it," she said.

I opened the box and inside was a beautiful dress, Guess what color? The same colors I'd admired in their bathroom two weeks before, turquoise and tan.

I cried as I held up the dress. It made me understand that much more how much God cares about even the little things. I thanked her. I told her how I was just admiring those same exact colors in her bathroom when we last visited her.

"Delight in the Lord and he will give you the desires of your heart," Psalm 37:4

I was so blessed by the dress, but what blessed me more was that God was revealing his love to me. He wanted me to know that he sees my heart and loved me enough to care. And though no one else knew, God knows even the very intent of our minds and hearts. God never ceases to amaze me!

"And Solomon, my son, learn to know the God of your ancestors intimately. Worship and serve him

with your whole heart and a willing mind. For the
LORD sees every heart and knows every plan and
thought. If you seek him, you will find him. But
if you forsake him, he will reject you forever."
1Chronicles 28:9 NLT

Abundant Gifts

One day, I was closing my car door when my
bracelet got caught on the hinge of the door somehow
and it broke my bracelet. It was 10k gold so I felt a
little bad, it was the only nice piece of jewelry that I
had. To someone else they may not have considered
it nice, but it was to me. It was one of those things
where you were so used to wearing it, you felt bare
without it. It wasn't something that I talked about to
anyone and it wasn't like I was losing sleep over it,
I was just a little disappointed.

A few weeks later we went to another friends'
house. A group of us were playing music and
worshipping the Lord together. We started praying
and after a short time of prayer, I felt someone take
my hand. As I opened my eyes I saw one of the girls
were wearing two gold bracelets take one of them
off and put it on my wrist.

As she was closing the clasp on it for me, she
said, "The Lord wants you to know that he loves
you" The message that the Lord loved me meant
more to me than the bracelet but it sure made the
bracelet more special than the one I had that broke.
And I thought it was interesting that the one I lost

was 10k gold and the one I received was 14k gold. Isn't that just like God?

God's love is so overwhelming. Some people may think it means that God will give you anything you want without an understanding of delighting in God. Delighting in God is trusting and committing your all to him. As we delight in him, if our heart is sincere, it will be toward him allowing the power of the Holy Spirit to mold us by his power into his likeness. God will give us the desires of our heart if we obey him, but we should not serve him for what we can get from him but because we love him.

"We love him because he first loved us." 1 John 4:19

Jesus said, "You shall love the Lord your God with all your heart,

all your soul and all your mind." This is the first and great commandment. And second is: You shall love your neighbor as yourself. These two commandments sum up all the law and the prophets." Matthew 22:37-40

If we follow these two commandments, the Ten Commandments would be covered, that's why the Scripture says these two sum it up.

"Now to him who is able to do exceedingly abundantly above all that we ask or think, according to the power that works in us, to him be glory in the church, by Christ Jesus to all generations, forever and ever, Amen." Ephesians 3:20-21 NKJV

"Delight in the Lord and he will give you the desires of your heart." Psalm 37:4

The Power in the name of Jesus

As I started learning more about the power we have in the name of Jesus, I found it to be very interesting. I was working in a restaurant in Chicago as a waitress. I was new there so I would get stuck with customers others didn't want to wait on.

A man came in, as soon as he came in you could hear all the other waitresses whispering and complaining. "I'm not waiting on him," they would all say.

"He makes you run back and forth and doesn't leave you any tip. We bring him his soup, go back for his salad, then his dinner and he keeps asking for other things at different times. He runs us ragged."

He'd been coming in for years and had never left a tip for anyone. It wasn't like he didn't have the money because he always ordered the most expensive meals.

They sat him in my station. I brought him his menu and could sense the presence of a stingy spirit. I went into the rest room and I prayed," I bind every selfish spirit away from me and my station in the name of Jesus Christ. Whatever you bind on earth shall be bound in Heaven." Matthew18:18.

Then I thanked the Lord that whatever I put my hand to prospers, and prayed in the spirit. Then I went to take his order. He ordered a big dinner. He did keep having me run back and forth as the others said he did.

When he left, I heard the other waitresses say, "Oh my gosh, I can't believe it, look on the table, he left a tip!"

They were shocked that he had left a tip at all, let alone a dollar which was a good tip back then. They couldn't understand why, when they worked there so many years, he wouldn't leave anything for them. They kept telling me how they couldn't believe it. I explained to them how I went into the bathroom and prayed and came against the selfish spirit. Then it was interesting, because he never came back again. I guess he didn't want to give up that selfish spirit.

I was so blessed that God being in our life can make things so much more exciting and interesting and how he's faithful to watch over his word even when it comes to these kind of things. "Then said the Lord to me, for I am alert and active, watching over my word to perform it." Jeremiah 1:12 Amplified

"God is not a man that he should tell or act a lie, neither the son of man, that he should feel repentance or compunction {for what he has promised}. Has he said and shall he not do it? Or has he not spoken and shall he not make it good?" Numbers 23:19 Amplified

CHAPTER 5

How Could I Forgive?

Icontinued reading the Word, and going to church where they didn't teach us about religion. I was tired of religion. It felt so nice to go somewhere where people from all religious backgrounds finally realized it's not about a religion but a relationship with God. I believe that in the last days, God's church will become one. It's exciting to see that it's happening already, people of all religious backgrounds coming together. To realize that we are not just people who go to churches but that we are the church.

"We are his house." Hebrews 3:6

Jesus' body ascended into Heaven and we are his body here on earth. We are his hands, we are his feet, and we are his lips. Before Jesus ascended into Heaven, he said, "I am telling you nothing but the truth when I say it is profitable good, expedient, advantageous for you that I go away. Because if I don't go away, the comforter Counselor, helper, advocate, Intercessor, strengthener, standby will not come to you into close fellowship with you; but if I go away, I will send him to you to be in close fellowship with you." John 16:7 Amplified

We are aliens because our citizenship is from above, from Heaven. The Bible says, "Our citizenship is in Heaven. And we eagerly await a Savior, from there, the Lord Jesus Christ." Philippians 3:20-21 NIV

"This is what the Lord says: He who created you, he who formed you, fear not, for I have redeemed you; I have summoned you by name; you are mine." Isaiah 43:1 NIV

"The people I have formed for myself, they shall show forth my praise." Isaiah 43:21 NIV

"Since you are precious and honored in my sight, and because I love you, I will give men in exchange for you, and people in exchange for your life." Isaiah 43:4 NIV

Though my earthly father was gone; I came to know my Heavenly Father.

God said he's a father to the fatherless. Psalm 68:5

My True Comfort

It was such a comfort to me to know that God cared for me and that he would watch over me.

As I continued to seek God by reading the Bible, and praying I grew closer to him. From past experiences so many religions believed you should do their religious things, and follow their religious rules. I wanted to know what God had to say. It was so refreshing to find the truth. And the truth was setting me free. God started dealing with my heart about forgiveness. I knew that according to the Bible he said I needed to forgive to be forgiven. It wasn't an easy thing to do because it's natural as human beings to feel like you're entitled to or have a right to hold unforgiveness.

I started to realize that just as a parent will tell their child something for their own good, God knew that forgiving was for my own good. I was only hurting myself, and it was time to get free. To be or not to be, that was the question: to be a forgiver or not to be a forgiver. We have a choice. I went down my list of all the people that had said or done wrong to me. I said, "Okay God, I forgive this person for this thing, and that person for that petty thing. I forgive my sister in law for putting me down all the time.

Then I got to the big one. I said, "My stepfather?" How could I? No, I can't do it. I knew I couldn't do it. There was no way I could. How could it be possible? But then I was reminded of the Scriptures where Jesus said we're to walk even as he walked. He wouldn't say to do it if it weren't possible.

"We can do all things through Christ who gives us the strength." Philippians 4:11

The Bible says we must forgive if we want God to hear and answer our prayers. We are commanded to love one another. If we sin, it separates us from God and our prayers are hindered.

God started helping me to understand that in order for a person to be able to take another persons life, they are possessed by another spirit.

He also reminded me of the Scripture in Ephesians 6:10-12 "Finally, be strong in the Lord and in his mighty power. Put on the full armor of God so that you can take your stand against the devil's schemes."

"For our struggle is not against flesh and blood, not people, but against the rulers, against the authorities, against the powers of this dark world and against the spiritual forces of evil in the Heavenly realms."

So in other words, it's the spirits that come against you. Being angry at the people will not help. It's just another strategy of the enemy to destroy you. I couldn't get away from the words.

God kept reminding me of how we do not fight against flesh and blood (people). I was reminded of how the devil had given me such a hard time in my life.

I asked God what I could do in return. The Lord reminded me that since I have the nature of God now, I can forgive.

I was reminded of the Scripture that says the love of God is shed abroad in our hearts by the Holy Spirit. God helped me to understand that I needed to pray for my stepfather and that as I prayed for him that I was giving the devil a hard time. At first it was difficult because I had so many hurts, so I cried out to God and he heard me. He wrapped his arms of love around me and started ministering to me with his great love and healing compassion.

I thanked God for continuing to heal my heart and asked God to help me to love like he loves so I could see others through his eyes. I said, "I set my will to do your will, which is to forgive." I was also reminded that I now have been given power over all the power of the enemy. And how it was up to me to use the power I have in the name of Jesus and use the word of God.

I could then have victory, or by listening to the lying thoughts of the enemy I could have defeat. I was reminded of how even Jesus was lied to by the devil and how by speaking the word he had victory. The word says that the Holy Spirit will put us in remembrance of all things that we need to be reminded of.

Praying for my Stepfather

The more we read God's word the more the Holy Spirit will remind us of the words we need to guide us in our life. As I prayed daily, I would also pray for my stepfather. God started helping me to understand that the devil hates all of us and wants all of us to go to Hell. He also started helping me to understand that Jesus paid that terrible price on the cross through the shedding of his blood for all of our sins, including my stepfathers.

I was reminded of the Scripture of how he that hates his brother is the same as a murderer, that sin is sin. 1 John 4:20.

After a few weeks went by, I started feeling a love as I was praying for my stepfather, a love I didn't feel for others. It wasn't natural, but supernatural!

Have you ever had the experience of being at church, where someone brought up a baby that was sick or dying and asked for you to stretch out your hands to pray for it? Well, if not, I'm sure you can imagine.

I remember how I felt such love, how my heart went out to it, thinking, oh, such a pure innocent baby.

Well, that's how I started feeling when I would continue to pray for my stepfather, as the Lord reminded me of the Scripture:

"Love covers a multitude of sins." 1st Peter 4:8

I was so happy that the Lord helped me to forgive him. God removed the bitterness and replaced it with a heart of love and compassion. I felt like a new person, with a new lease on life!

After I experienced this supernatural power of God in my life, I wanted to share it with others. The experience changed my life in such a dramatic way. I went through a lot in this race of life. If I hadn't put down the bags of bitterness, I would have given up the race and lost. I would have lost both my sanity and my life. By withholding forgiveness I would have chose to remain the victim. I came very close to giving up, because I grew weary carrying around the weight. It was like carrying a heavy burden that took all my strength. I could see no future for myself.

Forgiveness is not something I was able to do on my own. It flowed to and through me as I allowed God's love to flow to and through me. It took strength for me that only God could give me. I now know that God's word is true, and that we can do all things through Christ that strengthens us.

Sweet Revenge and Sweet Victory

I have found forgiveness to be "sweet revenge" and sweet victory. It really feels good! Forgiveness can be a challenge but it can help you see things differently. Forgiveness helps you so you can have the freedom to move forward. It can help you see that a better future awaits you. I wanted others to know that no matter what happens in life, we will be given opportunities in life to forgive or not to forgive and the choice we make will determine our quality of life.

I was able to share at a church one day how I was so thankful to God for helping me to forgive. I wanted people to know that if God can help me to forgive that God can help them to forgive also. Sometimes the devil is so subtle though that we don't notice it's him. A lot of trials that happen throughout our lives may seem trivial compared to other ones. And because of our lives sometimes becoming so busied, we tend to pretend that it's fine when we really have some issues we may need to deal with. That's why it's important to examine our hearts daily.

"Keep your heart with all diligence; for out of it are the issues of life." Proverbs 4:23

"Guard your heart above all else, for it determines the course of your life." Proverbs 4:23 NLT

Where your treasure is there will your heart be also." Matthew 6:21 NIV

"Out of the abundance of our hearts our mouths speak." Matthew 12:34 NKJV

As we think in our hearts so are we" Proverbs 23:7 NKJV

Your heart will be where your treasure is. The enemy will sneak into our hearts and lives by trying to get us to hold a grudge for this petty thing and that petty thing. Before you know it, all the petty things can add up and the cost will be at our expense.

At the expense of our health, our marriage, our success, happiness, and our peace. It can even effect our decision making which can result in what roads we take in life. Maybe the issues are within ourselves that are preventing us to walk in a higher realm of life. Sometimes fear, and wanting to be in control can hinder our walk. Sometimes pride, though we may not see it as pride, by wanting to live to please ourselves. Sometimes by ignoring our brokenness before God it results in feelings of guilt. A heart that is honest, right before God is what God delights in. Again, that's why it's important to examine our hearts daily.

"We need to be wise to the devils tactics. Be self controlled and alert. Your enemy the devil prowls around like a roaring lion looking for someone to devour." 1 Peter 5:8 NIV

Another good verse: "Do not give place to the devil." Ephesians 4:27

"If you harbor bitter envy and contention/selfish ambition in your hearts, there you will find disorder and every evil practice. This wisdom does not come down from above but is earthly, unspiritual, and even demonic." James 3:14-16 NIV

The devil's desire was that my step father would die and go to Hell, as his desire is for all of us. But Jesus paid the price for him as well as us.

Experience God's Love and Power

I want you to know that it's possible for you to experience God's love and power in your life daily. God loves you so much that he wants to have a relationship on a daily basis while you're here on earth and wants you for all eternity also.

You were created by him for him. It feels so nice to know that good could come out of the bad and that by exposing the devil for the thief that he is that others can find the truth and be set free also.

Jesus said "...you shall know the truth, and the truth shall make you free." John 8:32

We are assured and know that God being a partner in their labor all things work together and are fitting into a plan for good to and those who love God and are called according to his design and purpose. Romans 8:28 Amplified

CHAPTER 6

I See My Father's Murderer Again

"The thief comes only to steal, kill, and destroy; but Jesus said I have come that you might have life, and have it to the full." John 10:10 NIV

It was the enemies plan to continue to steal my peace, rob me of my happiness and to destroy me physically emotionally and financially. By my holding onto bitterness, it allowed the enemy to have a foothold in all these areas of my life.

I am so thankful that when we ask the Lord into our heart and life that his spirit, the greater one, lives within us and empowers us with his strength, with his nature, and his ability so we can live life to the full in every area.

"But you belong to God, my dear children. You have already won a victory over those people, because the spirit who lives in you is greater than the spirit who lives in the world." 1 John 4:4 NLT

"Beloved, I wish above all things that you prosper and be in health, even as your soul prospers." 3 John 1:2

I started to think about how bitterness is like a root and how it grows and just as a weed will strangle and destroy life around it unless it's removed, so will bitterness affect us and those around us.

"But if you harbor bitter envy and selfish ambition in your hearts, do not boast about it or deny the truth. Such wisdom does not come down from Heaven but is earthly, unspiritual, of the devil. For where you have envy and selfish ambition, there you find disorder and every evil practice." James 3:14-16 NIV

After I shared at a church about how God helped me to forgive my stepfather, I said maybe I'll see him again one day, and maybe I'll even have the opportunity to pray with him. I didn't know it would happen.

Preparations for Forgiveness

I prayed for him for seven years. Then one day I overheard my brother talking with my cousin about how his father, my stepfather was sick. As soon as I heard that, I heard God speak to my heart that I needed to go and see my stepfather. I talked with my husband and he was very supportive. When I asked my brother where his father lived he said he lived in a small town in Missouri.

He said." But don't go, not yet, wait ten days."
I'll be on vacation then and I can show you how to
get there.

I said, "No, I really feel like we should go right
away."

We knew that our old beater of a car would never
make the long trip. It was a seven to eight hour drive,
one way and we didn't have the money to go. We
asked a pastor to pray with us that God would give
us wisdom on how it would be possible. God laid it
on his heart to pay for a night stay at a hotel. Then
a friend of ours lent us her credit card so we could
rent a car to get there and back. It was a long drive
from Chicago to Missouri.

My husband did the driving and I climbed into
the back seat. I prayed in the spirit all the way
there. I hadn't a clue as to what I was to say when
I got there. I felt so far away from God. The Lord
reminded me of the Scripture that says not to give
any thought for what you'll say and that he would
fill my mouth. But I still felt so far away from God,
it made me feel bad. I couldn't understand why. I
said, "God, you know this isn't an easy thing for
me, why am I feeling so far away from you? I cried
out to God and continued to pray.

Later on I understood that it was an important
learning experience. It was a lesson that I would
learn from. When we arrived at the hotel where we
were staying I telephoned my stepfathers house. I
heard that he was remarried and that his wife was a
Christian woman. I thought that was pretty interest-

ing, I couldn't help but wonder if he had driven her to become a Christian. Anyway, when I telephoned their home she answered the phone. She had no idea we were coming.

Ready to face my Father's Murderer

I explained how I was Genes' stepdaughter and how I heard he was sick and that we were in town and would like to see him. She said he was sleeping but would be awake in a couple hours, so I said we'd see them then. We pulled up in front of the trailer court and saw him sitting in a chair out in front. As we got out of the car and started walking toward him, I saw him shaking his head back in forth in awe and unbelief. You have to remember the last time I had seen him was when I was in the court room testifying against him for my father's murder. I'm sure in the back of his mind, he was a little nervous. He was probably wondering if this was it, that we finally found him.

"I can't believe that you came all this way", he said. "I really feel bad about what happened but I want you to know I've been paying the price. I've been looking over my shoulder in fear every day of my life."

"How is everything, Do you have a family he asked?"

"Yes," I said, "but I'm really not here to chit-chat. I'm here because God told me to come here. The Lord wanted me to let you know that he's helped me to forgive you and that he has healed my heart. Most importantly, I want you to know that if you were to breathe your last breath right now, you would go right to Hell. And you said you've been paying the price, but Jesus is the one that paid the price. Jesus said that he that hates his brother is the same as a murderer, so in other words sin is sin. Jesus paid the price for your sin. There's a decision that you need to make in your life and if you'll sincerely ask the Lord to forgive you of your sins and come into your heart then your home will be Heaven. If you're ready to make that decision we'd like to pray with you."

He looked at his wife, Marge, and said, "I can't believe they came all this way to come and pray with me. What do you think Marge?"

And in her southern accent she said, "I think it's a good idea."

We all joined hands and prayed the prayer of salvation, and believe me, it was evident that God was there. As we were praying, God's love was so tangible, that his love came down like rain from Heaven. It was so amazing! Then Gene smiled a smile I had never seen before. And he said, "This changes everything."

Then God wanted to encourage me about how he hears our prayers and answers them though we may not always see the results. I had prayed for seven years prior to this day that everyday God would send someone across Gene's path. I prayed that he would come to know God's love for him and miss Hell and make Heaven.

Just as we started to get up to leave, his wife, Marge said, "Wait, I have to tell you something. Everyday God sent a pastor over to talk to Gene but he wouldn't listen. My sister sent him books on healing but he wouldn't read them, but God knew he'd listen to you."

I was so blessed that God made sure I heard those words to encourage me, to let me know that every day I prayed he heard my prayers and answered them. I can't find the words to tell you what an awesome experience it was. God gave me the privilege and honor of being his representative and it was sweet victory.

We went home and ten days later my stepfather died. In case you didn't remember, my brother had told me before we left to go see my stepfather to wait for ten days because he would be on vacation then and could show us how to get there. Well, it would have been ten days too late.

Don't Go by Feelings
And the lesson that God wanted me to learn by my feeling far away from him on the car ride there was not to go by feelings. We may not always feel spiritual but we can't always go by feelings. We need to learn and know the difference of hearing his voice, and how we could miss it if we went by feelings. We need to go by that still small voice, and be obedient to it no matter how we may feel and to remember that it can be a matter of life and death. I'm so thankful that God allowed me to experience

his great love in such a great magnitude and for also allowing me to have the pleasure of hurting the kingdom of darkness. I'm also so thankful for the godly husband that God gave me to stand by me during this time.

I pray that this story will help you to see that no matter what happens or has happened in your life that God is bigger!

Not too long after returning home from the trip to Missouri to see my stepfather, I heard a song on the radio. When I heard it, I couldn't believe how the words were so fitting. I immediately saw the music and words as background music to the end of the story. I pictured hearing the words in the background of the scene where we all held hands praying together and felt God's love come down like rain from Heaven. And after praying how Gene started shaking his head back and forth and said, "This changes everything."

Love Came Down

Everybody's got a story everybody's got a song
Everyone's a little different but we've all gone wrong
Then the Savior came and he took the blame
Changed everything

I could sing about his forgiveness
I could praise him till the sun goes down
I can say that I was a witness
I was there when his love came down
Love came down on me

Love broke through the darkness now I can
finally see
He paid the price for my freedom no more chains
on me
Since the Savior came and he took the blame
Changed everything
His love came down like rain from Heaven

Words and music by Lindell Cooley and Lenny
LeBlanc
If you buy this CD you will be blessed! It's called
One Desire-Available at: www.lennyleblanc.com

Everybody's' got a story. Whatever your story is,
God's interested in it. If it's a good story, thank God
for it. If it's a bad story, thank God that he can turn
it around for good.

"And we know that all things work together
for good to those who love God, to those who are
the called according to his purpose." Romans 8:28
NKJV

A Bright Future

You can have a bright future with God! Thoughts,
hurts, fears, bitterness and bad memories can prevent
you from being able to go forward in life. It's medically proven that these things can affect your mind,
body, and emotions. They can also affect the future
that God has intended for you.

I have learned from experience and through study
of God's word and prayer that though discourage-

ment tries to win you over, it doesn't mean that it's over. So many of us have listened to the spirit of discouragement that says there's nothing you can do, you just have to accept things the way they are, things will always be the same.

I used to be one of those people until I found a supernatural God who rescued me. I found hope when things looked hopeless. I found the way when it looked like there was no way. I wrote this book, not because I think I know it all, but because I found out the truth.

I pray you find the truth as well.

CHAPTER 7

What Lies ahead?

You can have a different outlook on life
Are you afraid to face another day?
Have you ever felt overwhelmed?

Did you ever have so much going on in your life and wonder if you could take much more? Did you ever wish there was more to life but thought it was too good to be true? I remember when I was younger how I felt. I thought about how nice it would be to just wake up and feel happy, not to have to go to a party or have a present given to me, but just to feel happy, just because. I didn't think it was really possible.

I've been there where life is hard and it makes it even harder when you think that God makes the bad things happen. It made me not want to have anything to do with God. When I thought about all the things I had been through and seen in my life, it made me picture God as being cruel. I didn't want to picture God as being cruel so I was convinced that he didn't exist. This was the truth that I knew, and this truth that I knew was really a lie that hurt a lot. The purpose of this book is to expose you to the truth. This truth can help you think differently so you can have a different outlook on life.

This truth can change the way you think, it can change your mind, your attitude, your heart, your health, and even your future.

It can affect your course in life as well as your eternal destiny.

The Truth Changes our Future

This truth changed my life dramatically and it can change yours too. I'm sure you've heard of the expression that the truth hurts, and sometimes it can. I'm sure you've also heard of how the truth can set you free. It is this truth that can set you free and that is what I would like to share with you.

Some people say that God makes bad things happen, and also some religions say God makes bad things happen.

But God's Word **says** in James 1:17, "Every good and perfect gift is from above and comes down from the Father of lights, with whom there's no variation or shadow of turning."

There's some good news that lies ahead.

God does not make the bad things happen, but he can help you through the bad times. And then again things are subject to change when you pray and believe according to God's will. What is his will? His word is his will. God's will is that you to be healthy and prosper.

"Beloved I wish above all things that you prosper and be in health, even as your soul prospers." 3 John 1:2

His will is that you have peace that this world can't give you.

"Do not be anxious about anything, but in everything, by prayer and petition, with thanksgiving, present your requests to God, and the peace of God which passes all understanding will guard your hearts and minds in Christ Jesus." Philippians 4:6-7

God's will is that you have long life. "With long life will I satisfy you and show you my salvation." Psalm 91:16 NKJV

God's will is to guide you and satisfy you. "The Lord will guide you continually, and satisfy your soul in drought, and strengthen your bones; you shall be like a watered garden, and like a spring of water, whose waters do not fail." Isaiah 58:11 NKJV

Some people have told me, "Oh, you can make whatever decisions you want in life, God doesn't care. He gives you a free will to choose as you may."

But the Bible says in all our ways to acknowledge him and he will direct our path. Why settle for less when you can have God's best? Instead of making good decisions, I'd rather make the best decisions when it comes time to decide on a job or a house, etc.

"All things work together for good for those who love the Lord and are called according to his purpose." Romans 8:28

A Hope and a Future

God's will is to give you hope and a future.

"For I know the plans I have for you," declares the Lord, " plans to prosper you and not to harm you, plans to give you hope and a future. Jeremiah 29:11

I'm reminded of the Scripture in John 10:10

It exposes the devil for who he really is.

"The thief which is the devil comes only to steal, kill, and destroy. But Jesus came to give us life and to give it to us more abundantly."

It means that Jesus came to give us a better than average life. It blesses me to think that the Lord loves and cares for us so much that he came to give us eternal life and that he wanted us to have an abundant life while here on earth.

So when life seems hard, and your relationships are being destroyed, and your life, health, finances are in jeopardy, and the devil is bombarding your mind with lying thoughts that God is to blame... remember, it's a lie. God is good.

As we look at the Lord's Prayer it also shows us that God is good. Jesus prayed: "Our Father, who is in Heaven, Holy is your name. Your kingdom come, your will be done on earth as it is in Heaven."

"In Heaven there is no sickness, so it's His will that we be healthy here on earth as they are in Heaven." Matthew 6:10

God wants us to live our life to the fullest in every area"Beloved, I pray that you may prosper in all things and be in health, just as your soul prospers." 3 John 1:2

It really blesses me to think that the Lord loves and cares for us so much that he wants to give us more…more than just an average life.

By knowing Jesus Christ, we can have a relationship in which God will literally guide our lives by the Holy Spirit through the Scriptures in the Bible, through prayer, church, and circumstances. That is why it is so important to get hooked up with a church that teaches the importance of learning the Scriptures from the Bible.

The Bible makes it very clear that it is our relationship with God through Jesus Christ, which saves us from Hell, and guarantees our home is Heaven. It is not religion but a relationship with God through Jesus Christ. Some people make a God out of their religion and think their religion is the way to Heaven, but God's word clearly tells you the way is through Jesus Christ. Jesus paid the price in full on the cross which redeemed us from our sin. He became sin for us that we might become the righteousness of God in him. Righteous means right standing with God. Getting our hearts right with God equals righteousness. His righteousness is like a robe upon us as referred to in Isaiah 61:10

Jesus answered, "I am the way and the truth and the life. No one comes to the father except through me." John 14:6

My Special Grandma

CHAPTER 8

Power in a Grandma's Prayers

One of the things that make grandparents unique in life is the impact of their presence and their influence in our lives. I consider myself to not only be fortunate but blessed because I had a grandmother that was a godly example. My grandma, Helen, believed God's word. She stood on this Scripture... "Believe on the Lord Jesus Christ, and you will be saved, you and your household." Acts 16:31

She's in Heaven now, but her prayers don't have an expiration date. They're still working! It's been exciting to see the results of her prayers over the years! Those results will definitely be stories for another book. My grandma took me with her to church on several occasions, when I was a little girl. Since my mother never took me to church, my grandma was my only connection to God. I remember seeing people falling on their face, crying out to God, and seeking his face.

Grandma is in Heaven now but her prayers don't have an expiration date!

Though at that time I didn't understand it all; I do remember experiencing the power of God. I have memories of my grandma every day sitting in her big chair with her big black Bible on her lap, meditating. I can remember how the countenance of her face would change after she had spent time with God. I could see that she received strength and peace as she put her trust in God.

It reminds me of the Scripture in Philippians 4:7 where it says, "And the peace of God which passes all understanding will guard your hearts and minds in Christ Jesus."

I felt like I could kind of relate with Timothy in the Bible because as he was growing up he had a father that was Greek that wasn't a believer and so did I. Acts 16:1

He also had a grandmother named Lois that had a sincere faith. Though I grew up in a negative environment the positive impact of my grandma, Helen's sincere faith helped me to remember that in spite of my circumstances in life there is a God that's bigger than my circumstances. 2 Timothy 1:5, 2 Timothy 3:12-15, Acts 16:1

Once in awhile, when I would start missing my father, I'd cry out to God and he would comfort me. "God is the Father of compassion and God of all comfort." 2 Corinthians 1:3

My son was ten years old now and I thought about how nice it would have been if my father and my son could have met each other. I then thought about how nice it would be if my son could go to Greece and meet my father's father, his great grandfather. Not long after that I received a letter from Greece from my grandfather. In the letter he said he would like for me to come to Greece and bring my son, so they could meet each other. He said he would pay for our roundtrip tickets. I was so thankful for his love and generosity and so thankful to God for speaking to his heart.

I was so thankful that once again God had intervened! Since my grandfather was an extension of my father it was a very special time that God had planned. They had a lot of bonding time. As we delighted in the Lord, he gave us the desires of our hearts. Psalm 37:4.

Thank you Lord, you overflow us with your love.

A Real Shepherd and Sheep

While we were there, we were driving on roads in the mountains. As we were driving, a Shepherd and his flock of sheep started to cross the road we were on, so we stopped. There were so many sheep that it took a little time for him to gather them and guide them in the right direction. It seemed funny, instead of waiting for a train to go by as we were used to in America we had to wait for the Shepherd and sheep to go by.

What an awesome sight, to see a Shepherd and his sheep in real life when I had only seen them before in pictures! It was a beautiful experience. I was very excited, so I asked if we could get out of the car. We were able to get out and talk with the Shepherd and pet some of the sheep and get some video footage. Of course I was reminded of the great Shepherd, Jesus.

Though Psalm 23 seems to be a favorite at funerals, it's not a Psalm of death. It's a Psalm of life, rest, and peace.

"To him the doorkeeper opens, and the sheep hear his voice; and he calls his own sheep by name and leads them out. And when he brings out his own sheep, he goes before them; and the sheep follow him, for they know his voice." John 10:3-4

The good shepherd leads and guides his sheep. He is their sole provider. He leads them into safe pastures to feed them, and brings them to places of rest and peace. He calms them, brings them to water so they can drink, tends to their wounds, and rescues them from pitfalls.

Jesus said, "I am the good shepherd; and I know my sheep, and am known by my own." John 10:14

The good Shepherd lays down his life for the sheep." John 10:11 NIV

If necessary a shepherd would risk his own life for the protection of the sheep. I saw the rod that the Shepherd carried for protecting the sheep from its predators. It was never used on the sheep but the staff was used to gently direct the sheep in the way they should go, I could see that the Shepherd cared and took his job serious. He called them and they listened because they were his sheep and they knew his voice.

Now may the God of peace who brought up our Lord Jesus from the dead, that Great Shepherd of the sheep through the blood of the everlasting covenant make you complete in every good work to do his will, working in you what is well pleasing in his sight, through Jesus Christ, to whom be glory forever, and ever, Amen. Hebrews 13:20-21 NKJ

So many of us have put our trust in certain things or people but the Bible says "Commit to the Lord whatever you do, and your plans will succeed" Proverbs 16:3

As we give Jesus Christ his rightful place as Lord over our life he will take us on the right path and lead us to places of rest. If you truly come to know the Lord Jesus as your Shepherd you will hear his voice and follow his ways and his promises will be yours to enjoy: You will not lack, he'll lead you to rest, and he'll refresh and restore your life and protect, guide and comfort you.

Your cup will run over. His goodness, mercy and unfailing love will follow you all the days of your life and his presence shall be your dwelling place. **"What do you think? If a man has a hundred sheep, and one of them goes astray, does he not**

leave the ninety-nine and go to the mountains to seek the one that is straying? And if he should find it, assuredly, I say to you, he rejoices more over that sheep than over the ninety-nine that did not go astray. Even so it is not the will of your Father who is in Heaven that one of you should perish." Matthew 18:12-14

Since David was a shepherd at one time he was familiar with the relationship between the sheep and the shepherd and wrote the twenty third Psalm.

One of mine and my Grandma's Favorite Psalms

Psalm of David-Psalm 23
Amplified

"The Lord is my Shepherd [to feed, guide, and shield me], I shall not lack. He makes me lie down in [fresh, tender] green pastures; He leads me beside the still and restful waters.

"He refreshes and restores my life {myself}; He leads me in the paths of righteousness [uprightness and right standing with Him-not for my earning it, but] for His name's sake."

Yes, though I walk through the [deep, sunless] valley of the shadow of death, I will fear or dread no evil, for you are with me; your rod [to protect] and your staff [to guide], they comfort me.

You prepare a table before me in the presence of my enemies. You anoint my head with oil my [brimming] cup runs over.

Surely or only goodness, mercy, and unfailing love shall follow me all the days of my life, and through the length of my days the house of the Lord [and His presence] shall be my dwelling place.

It is difficult for those living in a temperate climate to appreciate, but it was customary in hot climates to anoint the body with oil to protect it from excessive perspiration.

When mixed with perfume, the oil imparted a delightfully refreshing and invigorating sensation. Athletes anointed their bodies as a matter of course before running a race.

As the body, therefore, anointed with oil was refreshed, invigorated, and better fitted for action, so the Lord would anoint His "sheep" with the Holy Spirit, Whom oil symbolizes, to fit them to engage more freely in His service and run in the way He directs—in Heavenly fellowship with Him.

Help for the Hurting

I'll never forget when I was younger, though an adult, I would get

headaches, sometimes that were so bad I didn't know what to do. Nothing helped and I would telephone my grandma. Many times it was late at night, yet she would drive over and pray for me. She knew the power and authority that she had in the name of

Jesus over the enemy and she would get so mad at the devil and pray for me and I would be healed of the headache. Luke 10:19

I had battles with migraine headaches for many years but thank God I've been delivered from them. I can't remember the last time I had one. I can't find the words to express how thankful I am! If you've experienced the pain, I'm sure you know why I'm so thankful.

If you experience the problem now, God is still in the miracle working business. God is not a respecter of persons. What he does for one he'll do for another. The Lord loves you and wants to help you in every area of your life. Nothing is too small and nothing is too big. There is help for the hurting.

Jesus Christ came to seek and save the lost and he came to heal the broken hearted.

Whether you are hurting spiritually, physically, emotionally, or financially, he is more than willing and able to help you. The Lord is our helper. Let us then approach the throne of grace with confidence, so that we may receive mercy and find grace to help us in our time of need. Hebrews 4:16 NIV

God Cares for Me

My grandma always reminded me that God cares about us, and everything about us. She explained how he even cared about the little things.

She explained to me how she had to walk miles everyday to get water and then have to pump it and how she had to wash all their clothes on a scrub board.

There was so much work for her to do preparing and caring for her family. She told me how one day she had washed and hung the clothes to dry. She said after they dried that she had taken the socks down and was going to mend them because they had holes in them. They could not afford to go buy more socks like people do nowadays. When she took the socks off the line they no longer had holes in them. She said the holes were no longer there because God had miraculously mended them.

I was skeptical at first and said, are you sure someone else didn't replace the socks or mend them for you. She said no. It seems hard to believe when your mind is used to thinking naturally. But she believed in the supernatural power of God and the Bible does say "with God all things are possible."

The things that are impossible with people are possible with God.

But Jesus looked at them and said, "With men this is impossible, but all things are possible with God." Matthew 19:26

We Can Draw Closer To God

I thought about how the more time we spend on a relationship, for example in a marriage. If it's a good relationship as we draw closer to them, we give our love to them and it is given back to us. The more time we spend with the individual, we feel closer and grow to know them more. If we draw back or break our relationship by walking in unforgiveness, or dishonesty it puts a distance between us and we no longer feel the closeness we once had. As we apologize we are able to restore the broken fellowship and once again feel closer. As I spent more time with God I found the same to be true. As we draw nearer to him he draws nearer to us. God is love and in the beginning was the word and the word was with God and the word was God. If I sinned, and didn't get my heart right immediately with God, it broke our fellowship and I couldn't feel the closeness any longer. But the Bible makes it clear not to run from God, he is always waiting with open arms for us longing to draw us closer to him. His love is unconditional. Nothing can separate us from his love. Since we are human, we're not perfect but the Bible has the answer for that problem.

"My dear children, I write this to you so that you will not sin. But if anyone does sin, we have one who speaks to the Father in our defense-Jesus Christ, the righteous one. He is the atoning sacrifice for our sins, and not only for ours but also for the sins of the whole world." 1 John 2:1-2-NIV

The more time I spent meditating in the word and in worship and praise the more I experienced the supernatural love of God.

My Secret Hiding Place

When I was a little girl I stayed by my grandmas house. I would look forward to running to my secret hiding place. At the end of the block there was a huge empty lot that sat far back where a house had once stood. All that remained was the foundation, the rock which used to surround the diameter of the house. In the center and surrounding area were weeds and tall grass. Sometimes I would run there to get away from the noise and use my imagination. The rock was hard so I would pick a bunch of grass and lay it on the rock and pretend it was a couch and then lay down. I would imagine it was a house of my own. I'd close my eyes and it felt so good to feel the warmth of the sun shining down on me. It felt safe but it wasn't real and it was only temporary. When I heard my grandma yell for me I had to leave and come back to reality. After I grew up and came to the knowledge of the truth I found that Jesus the son of God was a reality. I found that he was my hiding place. That he was always and forever shall be. That he is the alpha and the omega, the beginning and the end. I found that he would surround me and protect me. He was my rock. I found that he was my firm foundation. That whenever I was afraid I could trust in him and he would protect me. I found that I could always count on him being there.

Keep your lives free from the love of money and be content with what you have, because God has said, "Never will I leave you; never will I forsake you." We can say with confidence, "The Lord's my helper; I won't be afraid. What can man do to me? Hebrews 13:5-7 Some people say that money is the root of all evil, thinking that they are quoting the bible. But that's not what the bible says. The bible says that the love of money is the root of all evil.

Having money is not evil, but loving it, lusting after it, and hording it is the evil.

Psalm 91 "The Lord is my rock, my fortress and my deliverer; my God is my rock in who I take refuge.

"The name of the Lord is a strong tower, the righteous runs into it and is safe." Proverbs 18:10

"You are my hiding place; you will protect me from trouble and surround me with songs of deliverance." Psalm 32:7 NIV

"When I am afraid I will trust in you" Psalm 56:3 NIV

"You are my refuge and my shield; I have put my hope in your word." Psalm 119:114 NIV

As I dwelled in that secret place of the most high he covered me with his feathers and under his wings I trusted.

"He is my shield and the horn of my salvation, my stronghold."

"Psalm 18:2 NIV

Remember when the enemy tells you to run the other direction, that's the voice of a stranger you should not follow. Run into the Fathers arms.

His sheep follow him because they know his voice. But they will never follow a stranger; in fact, they will run away from him because they do not recognize a strangers' voice. John10:4-5

Prayer Makes the Difference

As I grew older I remember getting my first ticket for speeding. I was very nervous since it was my first ticket and had never been to court before. My grandma told me that she would pray for me. She said remember that the Bible says when we obtained salvation that we also obtained favor with God and all people. Then she told me the story about how the heart of the King is in God's hand and he can turn it whichever way he wants and how I could ask for mercy- Proverbs 21:1 Well, it worked, God did show me mercy and the judge showed me mercy by dismissing it! I was impressed with knowing God and thankful for his love and mercy that endures forever. My grandma was happy too to see that prayer made a difference. I believe with all my heart that if it weren't for my grandma's prayers, I would probably be dead, insane or both. I know that I was in her prayers, and she always prayed for our family as well as for so many others.

I believe all of our family as well as many friends will see the salvation of God one day as a result of those prayers. As I look back at the memories of my grandma and her faith, I'm reminded of a grandma that loved me, a God that loved me and of a God that was bigger than any problem or anything in my life.

My grandma's house was like a haven of safety for me as I was growing up, until one day something very terrible happened, in the very same house where I once felt safe. My grandma no longer wanted to live there anymore, so she moved. I was so glad that she felt that way because it was a terrible reminder of the tragedy that took place there.

After seeing my father's murder I had come to a place in my life where I said to myself, "Why would

God let me go through the things I've been through and make me see what I've seen? It is then that I knew that my grandma was praying for me. I'm so thankful for my grandma's prayers; they made a difference in my life, so I would finally be open to see the truth. Then when I heard that God didn't make the bad happen but he can help you through the bad, and that through prayer things can change; I began to have a different outlook on God and started to become more interested in hearing more about him. Maybe it was a grandma that prayed for you, or a mother, or maybe a friend.

Maybe you are a grandma. If so, be encouraged, because a grandma's prayers can be powerful!

"The effective, fervent prayer of the righteous avails much." James 5:16 In verse 17 it says," <u>Elijah was a man</u> with a nature as ours, and he prayed earnestly that it would not rain; and it did not rain on the land for three years and six months." In verse 18 it states that "he prayed again, and the Heaven gave rain, and the earth produced it fruit." This is just one example of the power of God released through prayer.

Faith in prayer can change the course in our lives as well as nations. 2 Chronicles 7:14

Give up Fear

Whatever the reason, whether you come to God out fear of death, fear of life or fear of going to Hell… whether you're tired of trying to make it from day to day, or paycheck to paycheck…if you're tired of being so tired, then come to him and find rest. God doesn't care what the reason is; he's always longing to hear from you because he loves you.

"Jesus says: Come to me, all you who are weary and burdened, and I will give you rest." Matthew 11:28

"He gives power to the faint; and to them that have no might he increases their strength." Isaiah 40:29

"God demonstrated his own love toward us, in that while we were still sinners, Christ died for us." Romans 5:8

"For God so loved the world that he gave his only begotten son that whoever believes in him will not perish but have everlasting life." John 3:16

I used to try to fill the void inside of me just like so many other people do with things that still left my spirit empty. Neither alcohol, drugs, nor anything else was able to fill that void. My mind was so depressed. My heart was filled with such hurt, fear and despair.

The Bible states that we are created in the image of God, which means that God is a spirit. You are a spirit created to have fellowship with the spirit of the living God through Jesus Christ. That's why no one else and nothing else can satisfy our spirit.

Then I heard that Jesus Christ was the Prince Of peace, and that he was the healer of the broken hearted. "He is our peace that has broken down every wall." Ephesians 2:14

It was only his perfect love that could drive away my fears, heal my heart, and satisfy the longing in my soul.

Psalm 147:3 says "he heals the brokenhearted."

God can drive away your fears, heal your heart, and satisfy your deepest longing. Will you take hold of God's promise for you today?

CHAPTER 9

Free to be Confident

Growing up in an alcoholic home made it very hard to have any self esteem. It went beyond the phrase "children should be seen and not heard." We were rarely given the freedom to speak unless spoken to, and we were never to speak at the dinner table until everyone was finished eating. We seldom spoke for fear of saying something wrong.

This inferiority (fear) was something that had become a part of me. It was something I had become accustomed to and didn't think I could be free from it. As a child, walking to school, it was very hard to hold my head up because of such low esteem. Sometimes I would make myself hold my head so high to compensate that I was accused of being stuck up. But in reality, all I could think about was putting one foot in front of the other to get to where I was going.

As I grew up and even after I had married I still lacked self-esteem. So much so that I would rely on a drink to give me confidence when it really was a counterfeit for what God had to offer through a relationship with Jesus Christ.

As I started studying the word of God I found that it said, "Be not drunk with wine but to be filled with the spirit." Ephesians 5:8

The void inside that I once tried to fill with other things finally was filled by receiving the spirit of the Lord, and by drawing closer to him. I received what I really needed: righteousness, peace and joy.

"For the kingdom of God is not a matter of eating and drinking, but of righteousness, peace, and joy in the Holy Spirit." Romans 14:17

Now instead of reaching for a drink, I drink of the spirit of God and have a deeper and more satisfying experience.

Instead of relying on a drink, I rely on God to be my confidence, my comforter, and my friend through reading the Bible and praying. When I read His word I feel peace and joy increase in my life, like a supernatural high.

Nothing like the Real Thing

All I'm trying to tell you is that, "There's nothing like the real thing." Nothing can compare.

"As Jesus was praising the Father, the Lord of Heaven and earth, it states that Jesus was full of joy through the Holy Spirit." Luke 10:31

We also can experience this same joy through the Holy Spirit as we praise him. It is possible to live in a higher realm through the spirit of Jesus Christ.

I had a hunger that I found was being satisfied by reading and hearing the word of God.

I also found as I spent more time in his presence joy and strength increased in my life.

God is my Confidence

When I found out that God's word says that he is our confidence, I started to thank God. I said, "Thank you God that you are my confidence", it really started changing the way I felt. Each day as I would pray, I would thank him again and I became more and more free. As I meditated on Scriptures from the Bible, they would move from my mind to my heart and it started changing me. One of my favorites is:

"In the fear of the Lord is strong confidence: and his children shall have a place of refuge." Proverbs 14:26

I'm so thankful that I'm free from fear, that I'm free to be me, without having to have a drink or another vice to be my crutch.

One day as I was driving to work I was reminded of one of the first things that I had noticed and admired about my husband Kirk, when I first met him. As I rode along with him on his vending route for work one day I noticed that he always held his head up high and acknowledged everyone along the way with a friendly smile. I admired the confidence that he had.

It left an impression on me but I never really thought about it until I started writing this book.

I believe that God started helping me to understand that though Kirk's mother didn't have much, and it wasn't easy for her to raise her four children, she did have a great love for them and how that love made a difference. It was very evident that she loved and deeply cared for her children by what she said and by her actions. It is love that made a difference and gave them confidence and self-esteem. I thank God for giving me the privilege and honor of having his mother, Sally in my life.

She was like a mother to me. God helped me see that her love was like a seed that was planted in their hearts and confidence grew from it.

And in spite of the kind of home you came from God can make the difference in your life because God is love, and his love is the greatest power of all.

One morning God spoke to my heart and said, "When you are reminded of the many times that your mother spoke those hurtful words to you, remember that I am your Father and that you are loved by me, unconditionally. I love you with an everlasting love and as you grow in your understanding of my love for you, your heart will become as a well watered garden." He reminded me of this beautiful Scripture

"And the Lord shall guide you continually and satisfy you in drought and in dry places and make strong your bones. And you shall be like a watered garden and a spring of water of whose waters fail

not." Isaiah 58:11 Amplified It was such a comfort to me.

As I was writing this book, I felt led one day to call my sister in-law and ask her a question. I explained how I was writing the book and as I thought about love, thoughts of her mother had come to my mind.

I said to her, "Do you feel confident that your mother loved you?" She immediately said yes, I asked her again, if she ever had any doubt that her mother loved her, and she said no. I told her I felt the same way about her mother. It really blessed my heart as I was reminded of the great love that Sally had for her children as well as for me. She wasn't perfect, none of us are, but she was a very special person. It was very evident to me by her actions and words that she loved her children very much.

As I felt led to make that phone call I had hoped that it had been a blessing for her to be reminded of her mother's love. I didn't really know that God would use that phone conversation for my benefit but it was interesting how God used it as a lesson for me to be still and know that he is God. He then allowed me to have the privilege of having a conversation with him.

God's Love for Me

As I went back to work on the book, God started ministering his love to me as I was sitting at my desk. He asked me the same questions that I had asked my sister in law, only in regards to his love for me. He said, "Do you feel confident that I love you?" And I said," yes." Do you ever doubt my love? I said no, I know beyond a shadow of a doubt that you love me. It has been your love that has sustained me, it has been your love that has healed me, it has been your love that protected me, it was your love that redeemed me, It was your love that created me and knew me before you formed me in my mother's womb. It was you that approved of me.

It was your love that has separated me, set me apart and consecrated me. Your love has appointed me. I could sense his sweet presence. I wept as I experienced the sweet presence of his love during this special time together... just the two of us.

His reply was that as I rest in him I will have confidence.

For thus says the Lord God, the Holy one of Israel:

"In returning to me and resting in me you shall be saved; in quietness and in trusting confidence will be your strength." Isaiah 30:15

How to Have Peace

"The fruit of righteousness will be peace; the effect of righteousness will be quietness and confidence forever."

I had hoped that my phone call to my sister in-law was a blessing when I reminded her of her mother's great love for her and the love that was so evident that she had shown to all.

God in return had me take time to meditate, and be reminded of his great love for me.

The eyes of the Lord are on those who fear him, on those whose hope is in his unfailing love. Psalm 33:18

I am so thankful for God's unfailing love. If you haven't experienced it, come on in, the waters fine! God's love is so wide, deeper than the ocean, and higher than the mountains.

As high as the Heavens are above the earth, so great is his love for those who fear him; Psalm 103:11

I am so thankful for God's unfailing love. If you haven't experienced it, come on in, the waters fine!

"Have mercy on me O God, according to your unfailing love, according to your great compassion blot out my transgressions." Psalm 51:1

"I trust in your unfailing love, my heart rejoices in your salvation. Psalm 13:5

"You are forgiving and good O Lord, abounding in love to all who call to you." Psalm 86:5

"Satisfy us in the morning with your unfailing love, that we may be glad all our days." Psalm 90:14

"Your love is better than life, my lips will glorify you." Psalm 63:3

"We love him, because he first loved us."
1 John 4:19 Amplified

"Who redeems our life from the pit and crowns us with love and compassion." Psalm 103:4

Think about God's unfailing love for you. Bask in it. Understand that His love is greater than the love of any human being. When you concentrate on the love of God, you will find that you will view the difficult circumstances of your life quite differently.

CHAPTER 10

You Have a Future with God

God has a plan and a purpose for your life.
How do we know what God's will is for our life? God's' word (Bible) is his will. The word of God (the Bible) is supernatural; the Bible does not consist of mere words as you would see in a book or newspaper. "God's word is spirit and life" John 6:63

"Do not conform any longer to this world, but be transformed by the renewing of your mind. Then you will be able to test and approve what God's will is-his good, pleasing and perfect will" Romans 12:2 NKJV

"For I know the thoughts that I think toward you, says the Lord, thoughts of peace and not of evil, to give you a future and a hope. Jeremiah 29:11 NKJV

Thoughts, hurts, fears, bitterness and bad memories can prevent you from being able to go forward in life. It's medically proven that these things can affect your mind, body, and emotions. They can also affect the future that God has intended for you. I have learned from experience and through study of God's word and prayer that though discouragement tries to win you over, it doesn't mean that it's over.

So many of us have listened to the spirit of discouragement that says there's nothing you can do, you just have to accept things the way they are, things will always be the same. I used to be one of those people until I found a supernatural God who rescued me.

Hope Even When Hopeless

I found hope when things looked hopeless. I found the way when it looked like there was no way. I wrote this book, not because I think I know it all but because I found out the truth. God doesn't make the bad happen in life but will help you through the bad. I know that God's love is unconditional and that nothing can separate us from his love. I know that his love is the greatest power there is and that his love never fails. I know God's unfailing love was a comfort to David Psalm 119:76 and his love is a comfort to me. Let God's love comfort you. By reading and meditating on the truths in this book God will reveal his love to you. Read the Bible as if it were a love letter from God. It really is to each one of us personally.

"If anyone be in Christ then they have become a new creation, old things are passed away and all things become new." 2 Corinthians 5:17

As we yield ourselves to him he will take our lives and help us to be the person that he created us to be.

Where there once was fear and inferiority there will be quiet and confidence. Where there once was worry and doubt, there will be peace that the world can't give you, a peace that passes all understanding. Where there once was lack, there will be no more. Where once there was darkness, there will be light. "God's' word is a lamp unto our feet and a light unto our path." Psalm 119:105

Your understanding of his love for you will deepen and you will "learn to live in a higher realm of life".

Where there were tears of sorrow, will be tears of joy. "Jesus came to make our joy complete." 1 John 1:4

My prayer for you is that by reading this book you will come to know the truth and will walk in it daily. There really is more to life, and that more is God. Through the reading of God's word you will come to know the creator of this universe in a deeper way. Your understanding of his love for you will deepen and you will "learn to live in a higher realm of life".

"The Lord Jesus Christ is our hope." Psalm 71:5

"Seek first God's kingdom and his righteousness and all these things will be added onto you." Matthew 6:33

Peace—"Therefore, since we have been justified through faith, we have peace with God through our Lord Jesus Christ" Romans 5:1

"May the God of hope fill you with all hope and peace as you trust in him, so that you may overflow with hope by the holy spirit" Romans 5:13   When you are serving God and walking in his ways, he will guide you, protect you, comfort you, and strengthen you.

"It is impossible to please God without faith. Anyone who wants to come to him must believe that God exists and that he rewards those who sincerely seek him." Hebrews 11:6

"Faith comes by hearing the word of God." Romans 10:17

"Our help is in the name of our Lord, who made Heaven and earth."

Psalm 129:8

"We can say with confidence, the Lord is my helper; I will not be afraid. What can man do to me?" Hebrews 3:6

"God is our refuge and strength, a very present help in times of trouble." Psalm 96:1

"The Lord is my strength and my song; he has become my salvation." Exodus15:2

"Yes, let us know recognize, be acquainted with, and understand him; let us be zealous to know the Lord, to appreciate, give heed to, and cherish him. His going forth is prepared and certain as the dawn, and he will come to us as the heavy rain, as the latter rain that waters the earth." Hosea 6:3 Amplified

"For I am persuaded that neither death nor life, nor angels nor principalities or powers, nor things present nor things to come, nor height nor depth, nor any other created thing, shall be able to separate us from the love of God which is in Christ Jesus our Lord." Romans 8:38

God knows you better than anyone, yet loves you more than any one.

"Greater love has no one than this, than to lay down ones life for a friend" John 15:13

"God even knows how many hairs are on your head." Matthew 10:30

"Don't be anxious and worried about your life, saying what shall we eat? Or what shall we drink? Or what will we wear? Look at the birds of the air, they neither sow nor reap nor gather into barns, yet your Heavenly Father feeds them." Matthew 6:25-26

"Consider the lilies of the field, how they grow, they neither toil or spin; now if God so clothe the grass of the field, which today is and tomorrow is thrown into the oven, will he not much more take care of you, O, you of little faith?" Matthew 6:30

In 1 Peter 5:7 it says "Cast all your cares upon God, for he cares for you."

"But seek first the Kingdom of God and his righteousness and all these things shall be added onto you" Matthew 6:33

When you are serving God and walking in his ways, he will guide you, protect you, comfort you, and strengthen you. "God rewards those

who earnestly seek him." Hebrews 11:6 NIV

Don't listen to those negative thoughts when they try to come against your mind, telling you that God doesn't really care. Those are lies from the enemy.

"The enemy which is the devil is the father of lies and a thief." John 8:44

"Submit yourselves, then, to God. Resist the devil, and he will flee from you." James 4:7

So when the thoughts that are contrary come to you, thank God for his word. "Thank him that he cares and tell him that you are casting all your cares upon him like he said to do." 1 Peter 5:7

Even Jesus had to deal with negative thoughts and words, but instead of agreeing with them, Jesus trusted in God's word and spoke the word. When Jesus was tempted by the devil, Jesus answered, "It is written: 'Man does not live on bread alone, but on every word that comes from the mouth of God." Matthew 4:4 NIV

He knew the word was full of power and wouldn't return void. See Matthew 4:10-11

The Bible says in 2 Corinthians 20:5 to "cast down every evil thought that exalts itself against the knowledge of God."

A How-To Manual for Your Life

A manual for your car gives you instruction on how to care for your vehicle. If you maintain it as instructed you will find that it will extend the life of your vehicle. You can learn what to do to prevent problems from arising. And when problems do arise it can help you find the answers you need. As you maintain your car by changing your oil regularly and getting tune ups, etc. it makes a huge difference resulting in less problems and more enjoyment. On the other hand if you don't have any knowledge about your vehicle and therefore don't maintain it, it will shorten the life of the vehicle and can destroy it.

The Bible is our manual for our life. It helps us so our lives can run more smoothly if we will follow the advice that is recommended. When you get thirsty it will quench your thirst. When you grow weary it will renew your strength. It will help you so not to feel anxious, and instruct you to take one day at a time, and to cast all your cares on God.

Words from the apostle Paul: "Be anxious for nothing, but in everything let your requests be known to God; and the peace of God which surpasses all understanding, will guard your hearts and minds through Christ Jesus." Philippians 4:6-7

"I wish above things that you prosper and be in health, even as your soul prospers." 3 John 2

It can help prolong your life. It will give you instruction as to what to do to live a richer, more productive life. It will inform you of the oil that will benefit you:

The oil of gladness Hebrews 1:9

We need to examine our hearts because out of it are the issues of life.

"The Bible says my people are destroyed because of lack of knowledge" Hosea 4:6

Our Wonderful Powerful Bible

There is so much knowledge that's in the Bible but it can't help us if we don't read it. As we read it we can gain wisdom and knowledge to help us in our lives in so many ways.

"Wisdom is the principal thing; therefore get wisdom: and with all thy getting get understanding." Proverbs 4:7

"How much better to get wisdom than gold and good judgment than silver!" Proverbs 16:16

"Wisdom of this world is foolishness to God. He catches the wise in their craftiness." 1Cor 3:19

"We do not cease to pray for you and to desire that you may be filled with the knowledge of his will in all wisdom and spiritual understanding." Colossians 1:9

The Bible tops the best seller list every year. World sales are more than a hundred million a year. It has been estimated that between 1815 and 1975 some 2.5 billion copies of the Bible were printed.

A more recent survey for the years up to 1992 put it closer to 6,000,000,000 in more than 2,000 languages and dialects. Whatever the precise figure, the Bible is by far the best selling book of all time. Think about it...

External evidence from both archaeology and non-Christian writers confirm the Bible-is a trustworthy historical document.

The fact that the Bible continues to change thousands of lives around the world in positive, tangible ways displays another clear proof of its inspiration by the Holy Spirit.

"All Scripture is given by inspiration of God, and is profitable for doctrine, for reproof, for correction, and for instruction in righteousness." 2 Timothy 3:16

Just as food nourishes our bodies, God word (the Bible) brings nourishment to our spirit, and wisdom and knowledge to our heart and minds.

"Jesus said we shall not live by bread alone, but by every word that proceeds out of the mouth of God." (the Bible) Matthew 4:4

Using God's word daily will allow it to work in our lives. Just as we need food daily, our spirit needs the word of God daily. Otherwise, we will grow weak, and not think clearly.

Jesus said," the words that I speak to you are spirit, and they are life" John 6:63

We were created to have fellowship with the spirit of the living God through Jesus Christ. That's why no one else and nothing else can satisfy our spirit.

"Faith comes by hearing and hearing by the word of God." Romans 10:17

"The word of God is quick, and powerful, and sharper than any two edged sword, piercing even to the dividing asunder of soul and spirit, and of the joints and marrow, and is a discerner of the thoughts and intent of the heart." Hebrews 4:12

"The sword of the spirit is the word of God." Ephesians 6:17

We were created in the image of God and God is a spirit. We are spirits that live in bodies. We need to feed our spirit with the Bible.

God's word is spirit and life. As we feed our spirit more than our body, our spirits will become stronger and more in tune to God.

"When you receive the message of God and welcome it not as the word of mere men but as it truly is, the word of God, which is effectually at work in you who believe (exercising its superhuman power in those who adhere to and trust in and rely on it)." 1 Thessalonians 2:13 Amplified Bible

"Though you have not seen Him, you love Him; and even though you do not see Him now, you believe in Him and are filled with an inexpressible and glorious joy." 1 Peter1:8

Then Jesus told him, "Because you have seen me, you have believed; blessed are those who have not seen and yet have believed." John 20:29NIV

"Since God inhabits our praises, that means our praising God brings down his presence." Psalm 22:3

"In the presence of the Lord there is fullness of joy." Psalm 16:11

"The joy of the Lord is your strength." Nehemiah 8:10

The joy that you can experience from being in the presence of God doesn't compare to anything else.

"Then make my joy complete by being like-minded, having the same love, being one in spirit and in purpose." Philippians 2:2

Famous Quotations

It is impossible to rightly govern the world without God and the Bible. –George Washington

I believe the Bible is the best gift God has ever given to man- All the good from the Savior of the world is communicated to us through this book. Abraham Lincoln 1809-1865 16th U.S. President

The Bible is the sheet-anchor of our liberties, — Ulysses S. Grant 1822-1885 18th U.S. President

A thorough knowledge of the Bible is worth more than a college education.— Theodore Roosevelt 1858-1919 26th President of the U.S.A.

The secret of my success — it is simple. It is found in the Bible- George Washington Carver

Of the many influences that have shaped the United States into a distinctive nation and people, none may be said to be more fundamental and enduring than the Bible. —President Ronald Reagan, 40th President of the United States

When you have read the Bible, you know it is the word of God, because it is the key to your heart, your own happiness, and your own duty.— —Woodrow Wilson, 28th President of the United States, 1856-1924

It has been my custom for many years to read the Bible in its entirety once a year. –John Quincy Adams U.S. president 1825-1829

Scriptures to Give You Strength

Here are some more great Scriptures to feed your spirit. As you read them aloud and meditate on them they will nourish your spirit, renew your mind and bring faith to your heart:

"Study this Book of Instruction continually. Meditate on it day and night so you will be sure to obey everything written in it. Only then will you prosper and succeed in all you do." Joshua 1:8

"But seek first God's kingdom and his righteousness and all these things will be added onto you." Matthew 6:33

The author of Psalm 119 wrote: "I have hidden your word in my heart that I may not sin against you."

David knew the importance of keeping a regular supply of God's word in his heart would help him to stay on the right path.

Renew Your Mind

Our spirits are made new when we receive Christ but our minds do not change. That's why we need to read God's word to renew our minds. Through reading the word, our minds will be changed to think differently. It will change our whole outlook. It will not only help us to think more positive which is good but as the word gets down into our hearts there lies the power that transforms our lives.

"Do not conform any longer to the pattern of this world, but be transformed by the renewing of your mind. Then you will be able to test and approve of what God's will is- his good, pleasing and perfect will" Romans 12:2

"Faith comes by hearing the message, and the message is heard through the word of Christ." Romans 10:17

Jesus says, "The words I speak to you are spirit, and they are life." John 6:63

The more we dwell on a thought, the more apt we are to act on it. That is why we need to dwell on God's word, so we will act on it instead of words or thoughts that would be contradictive to the word.

"Whatsoever things are true, whatsoever things are honest, whatsoever things are just, whatsoever things are pure, whatsoever things are lovely, what-soever things are of good report; if there be any virtue, if there be praise, think on these things. Those things both that you have learned, and received, and heard, and seen in me, do: and the God of peace shall be with you" Philippians 4:8-9

"But to as many as did receive and welcome Him, He gave the authority power, privilege, right to become the children of God, that is, to those who believe in adhere to, trust in, and rely on His name." John 1:12 Amplified

"If any person is in Christ he is a new creation a new creature altogether; the old previous moral and spiritual condition has passed away. Behold the fresh and new has come!" 2 Corinthians 5:17 Amplified

How does God play a part in what your future holds?

"By In all your ways acknowledging him, then he will direct your paths." Proverbs 3:6

"When you delight in the Lord he will give you the desires of your heart." Psalm 37:4

"For I know the plans I have for you, declares the Lord, plans to prosper you and not to harm you, plans to give you a hope and a future." Jeremiah 29:11

"Jesus said, I have come that you might have life and have it to the full." John 10:10

"Beloved, I wish above all things that you prosper and be in health, even as your soul prospers." 3 John 1:2

"Seek first the kingdom of God and all these things shall be added unto you." Matthew 6:33

"Blessed is the one that trusts in the Lord and whose hope is in the Lord." Jeremiah 17:7

"Do not be wise in your own eyes' fear the Lord and shun evil. This will bring health to your body and nourishment to your bones." Proverbs 3:7-8

Incredible Miracles from God

I remember one day I was getting a little frustrated because we needed food. We were thinking about asking someone if we could borrow some money until next week. I was so tired of borrowing, when the next week came we'd pay it back and be in the hole again, it seemed like a never ending cycle. I said, "No, God said he'd supply all of our needs, and that he's not a man that he'd lie" We shouldn't have to borrow the money. We decided we'd trust in the Lord and didn't tell anyone we needed food, except for God. We went to church the next morning and as we started to leave the service someone followed us as we were walking to our car. They asked us if we would be offended if they gave us some bags of groceries. We felt kind of funny at first but said, no, and thanked them for being a blessing to us. It brought tears to our eyes. We were so surprised because they didn't know us very well and they didn't know our likes and dislikes, yet all four bags of groceries had food in them that we would have bought ourselves. We were so thankful to them and to God for supplying the food through them. We were so blessed and will always remember how God showed himself to be faithful.

There was another time that we were struggling financially and were in desperate need of three hundred dollars to be exact to pay our rent. We didn't tell anyone but God heard our prayer and as we were leaving church one morning someone handed us an envelope and said God said to give this to you. We had seen the people at church before but we didn't know them otherwise and they didn't know of our situation, but God spoke to their heart and they were obedient to his voice. When we got in the car and opened the envelope and it had exactly three hundred dollars in it! God is so faithful!

"Don't be anxious and worried about your life, saying what shall we eat? Or what shall we drink? Or what will we wear? Look at the birds of the air, they neither sow nor reap nor gather into barns, yet your Heavenly Father feeds them." Matthew 6:25-26

"Consider the lilies of the field, how they grow, they neither toil or spin; now if God so clothe the grass of the field, which today is and tomorrow is thrown into the oven, will he not much more take care of you, O, you of little faith?" Matthew 6:30

"My God shall supply all your needs"- Philippians 4:19

"But seek ye first the kingdom of God, and His righteousness; and all these things shall be added unto you." Matthew 6:33

"For God so loved the world that he gave his one and only son, that whosoever believes in him shall not perish but have everlasting life" John3:16

"God did not send his son into the world to condemn the world, but that the world through him might be saved." John 3:17

"In the beginning was the word, and the word was with God, and the word was God. And the word became flesh and dwelt among us, Jesus and we beheld his glory, glory as the only begotten from the Father, full of grace and truth. Jesus said that his words are spirit and life" John 6:63

Build Your House on the Rock

Whoever hears these words and acts upon them obeying them will be a sensible prudent practical and wise person who built his house upon a rock. And the rain and the floods came and the winds blew and beat against that house' yet it did not fall, because it had been founded on the rock. And everyone who hears these words of mine and does not do them will be like a foolish person who built his house upon the sand. The rain fell and the floods came and the winds blew and beat against that house and it fell — and great and complete were the fall of it." Matthew 7:24-27

There's no power on this earth that can stand against God word. Build your house on the rock and it will stand!

"The Lord is my rock, my fortress, and my deliverer; my God, my keen and my firm strength in whom I will trust and take refuge, my shield, and the horn of my salvation, my high tower." Psalm 18:2 Amplified

"When the enemy shall come in like a flood, the Spirit of the Lord shall lift up a standard against him" Isaiah 59:19

"God's' word is a lamp unto our feet and a light onto our path." Psalm 119:105 NIV

Jesus answered" It is written: Man does not live on bread alone but on every word that comes from the mouth of God. Matthew 4:4 NIV

"Yet in all these things we are more than conquerors through Christ who loves us.

Romans 8:37 NKJV

The only weapon the devil has against a child of God is thoughts and it's up to us what we do with those thoughts. Even Jesus needed to use the word of God.

"Then Jesus was led, guided by the Holy Spirit into the wilderness desert to be tempted tested and tried by the devil.

And he went without food for forty days and forty nights and later he was hungry. And the tempter came and said to him, if you are God's son; command these stones to be made loaves of bread.

But he replied, it has been written, man shall not live and be upheld and sustained by bread alone, but by every word that comes forth by the mouth of God." Matthew 4:1-4 Amplified

When the thought or feeling comes to you that you are weak, remember God's word says, "Let the weak say I am strong" Joel 3:10

"The Lord is the strength of my life." Psalm 27:1

"Therefore do not worry about tomorrow, for tomorrow will worry about its own things. Sufficient for the day is its own trouble."

In other words, take one day at a time. "In all these things we are more than conquerors through him who loves us." Romans 8:37

"While we do not look at the things which are seen, but at the things that are not seen. For the things which are seen are temporary but the things that are not seen are eternal." 1Cor 4:18

"Jesus said whatever you ask the Father in his name according to his will shall be done." John 15:16

No matter what your circumstances may look like today, remember they are subject to change.

God is bigger than your circumstances.

How big is God?

He is so big that:

"God says Heaven is my throne, and the earth is my footstool." Isaiah 66:1

It's a great reminder of how great God is!

"All things are possible with God!"

Matthew 19:26

Take a moment right now to remember that all things are possible with God—especially during the dark days.

CHAPTER 11

Consider God's Word

The word "Consider" does not mean simply "to notice".

The word also means to give careful, studious attention to, to think about, intentional.

To examine, study, mentally ponder, reflect, meditate, and believe.

Dwelling on your circumstances can cause you to worry and fear.

Meditating on God's word will create faith and drive fear away.

"Dwelling on God's word will cause faith to rise in your heart, and cause your way to be prosperous and then you will have great success."

Joshua 1:8 NKJ

"Finally, brothers and sisters, whatever is true, whatever is noble, whatever is right, whatever is pure, whatever is lovely, whatever is admirable, if anything is excellent or praiseworthy, think about such things." Philippians 4:8

"Whatever you have learned or received or heard from me, or seen in me- put it into practice. And the God of peace will be with you." Philippians 4:9

Get Out from Under the Circumstances

Don't give in though it may be tempting to say, "I'm alright considering the circumstances." Or some might think they are alright under the circumstances.

We can get out from under the circumstances. As we administer the word to our spirit and mind, the word will rise up in our hearts, by believing and speaking it we will rise above our circumstances. Our circumstances are subject to change as we believe in the power of the word and apply it to our life. Consider God's word, not the circumstances. Walk by faith, not by sight. The things that are seen are temporal, but the things that are not seen are eternal. Let God reign over the circumstances.

We need to be reminded from time to time of what the word of God has to say, especially when circumstances seem to be speaking so loudly to us.

Remember he said "Consider the lilies of the field, God takes care of them and you are of much more value than them." Matthew 6:25-28

You are Precious and Valuable to Your Creator

You are precious and valuable in God's sight. He loves you with an everlasting love. Consider how much God loves you. He loves you so much that he sent his one and only son Jesus to die for you personally.

Consider how great God's love is. "Behold what manner of love the Father has bestowed on us, that we should be called the children of God!" 1 John 3:1Consider the fact that you were made in God's image and likeness, and he didn't make anything else in his likeness. Consider that there is no one else like you, you are unique. In life I've heard it said that it's not what you know but who you know.

Maybe you know some people in high places. But the creator of the universe is as high as you can go. God the creator of the universe He loves us and longs to have a relationship with you and made it possible through his son Jesus Christ. There is no other way to come to know him. Jesus said, "I am the way the truth and the life. No one comes to the Father except through me. John 14:6

Consider the fact that you were made in God's image and likeness, and he didn't make anything else in his likeness. Consider that there is no one else like you, you are unique.

I think one of the first things I consider when I think of God's love is

John 3:16. "For God so loved the world that he gave his one and only begotten son, that whoever believes in him should not perish but have everlasting life."

Consider the cost of the cross. When he carried it, we were on his mind.

When he bore the cross, we were on his mind. We are always on his mind.

The price was so great to save all the lost. Consider his body that was nailed on the tree and the blood that he shed to set us all free. The pain he endured, the great agony, no greater love could there ever be than when Jesus died on Calvary. No words could express the anguish when he laid down his life for us all. His blood that was spilled redeemed us from sin and gives us life eternally.

Peter writes, "Cast all your cares on God because he cares for you"

Consider the fact that God made the earth for us with all of its beauty. When I see a flower, I see the hand of God. He didn't have to go out of his way to make them but he did because of his love for us.

Wouldn't you think that a loving God would give us a manual for our life?

By his spirit he has. He inspired a book that has all the answers we need to help lead and guide us daily. The book is the Bible that has helped more than billions of people all over the world.

Open Your Spiritual Eyes
After you receive Jesus Christ your spiritual eyes will be opened to see things in it you didn't see before and it will change your heart, your mind and your future.

If you haven't asked Jesus to forgive you of your sins and come into your heart, now is the time, right where you are. The Bible says now is the time of salvation. Isaiah 49:8

I hear many people say, "Oh, I'm a good person, I never killed anyone" The Bible says we all have sinned and fallen short of the glory of God.

We've all sinned and we need to get rid of our pride and admit it, don't compare your self with this person or that person.

And yes, there's many times in life when we can definitely say life's not fair. That's why God sent Jesus to redeem us.

Jesus became our perfect sacrifice: his blood cleanses us from all our sins, as far as the east is from the west, never to be remembered again.

Sin separates us from God just as it did with Adam and Eve.

But Jesus is the bridge that will bring you back to God.

It's not religion that will get you to Heaven, but a relationship with God through Jesus Christ.

Religion is not the answer; it was religious people that killed Jesus.

Jesus became our substitute by dying in our place and taking all of our sins upon him when he died upon the cross; he suffered so we don't have to suffer.

It's not religion that will get you to Heaven, but a relationship with God through Jesus Christ.

Jesus said no one can come to the Father except through him. Jesus is the way, the truth and the life.

It's not good works that saves you as some religions may claim.

The cost was the cross, the price has been paid. The blood of Jesus will never lose its power. It speaks healing and forgiveness.

"By grace are you saved through faith, and not of yourselves, it is a free gift of God, not of works, lest anyone should boast." Ephesians 2:8 & 9 NIV

Jesus became our perfect sacrifice; his blood cleanses us from all our sins, as far as the east is from the west, never to be remembered again. Psalm 103:12

God loves you so much that he sent his Son to die for you. Let the truth of God's love change the way you live today.

CHAPTER 12

Are You Under a Curse?

Maybe you have wondered if you were under a curse because of things going on or not going on in your life. I know I used to wonder myself. I've also heard many other people in life say that they felt or wondered if they could be under a curse. Well the answer is yes, there is such a thing.

If you don't know Jesus Christ as your personal Lord and Savior, you are under a curse. But the good news is according to the Bible "Christ redeemed freed us from the curse by becoming a curse for us, for it is written: Cursed is everyone who is hung on a tree" Galatians 3:13

The book of Deuteronomy has a long list of curses. Sickness, poverty, shortened life and bareness are just a few of the curses. If you haven't asked Jesus Christ to forgive you of your sins and received him as your Savior, you are under a curse.

"I have set before you life and death, blessing and cursing; therefore choose life, that you and your descendants may live" Deut. 30:19

"Jesus said I am the way, truth and the life." John 14:6-9

"That you may love the Lord your God that you may obey his voice, that you may cling to him, for he is your life and the length of your days;" Duet 30:20

But when you make the decision of asking Jesus Christ to forgive you of your sins, you are redeemed from the curse. He came to set us free.

Jesus could have called down ten thousand angels to rescue him from the cross but he loved you so much that he chose to be obedient to death, even the death on the cross so that we might have eternal life through him by believing and receiving him into our hearts and lives.

As Jesus carried the cross down the road to Calvary you were on his mind.

It was Jesus love for you that held him on the cross that day. This knowledge will transform your thinking and cause you to understand just how much he loves you.

Our blessings are not always automatic though. As you read on, you will see conditions stated clearly throughout the Bible. If we want to be cursed, we could do nothing. If we want the blessings of God let us repent and turn from our ways. As we turn to God and give our all to him, he will give his all back to us. "Give and it will be given to you." Luke 6:38

"To obey is better than sacrifice" 1 Samuel 15:22

When people in the Bible obeyed God they received blessings, when they didn't obey, the opposite happened. I think a lot of the time people can have a problem with the word obey. Some may think of it as something negative. I know I've had the thought come to my mind that it sounds controlling for someone to want us to obey them. Really obeying is something you do, it's submitting. Of course, those thoughts will come. Those thoughts came to Adam and Eve and we know where they come from. The enemy even tempted Jesus to disobey God.

According to Webster's Revised Unabridged Dictionary the definition of obey is: 1. To give ear to; to execute the commands of; to yield submission to; to comply with the orders of; 2. To submit to the authority of; to be ruled by; 3.To yield to the impulse, power, or operation of; as a ship obeys her helm.

I think Genesis is a good place to start. Through Adam and Eve disobedience separated them from God, and as a result sin had dominion over all mankind. Our disobedience separates us from God and stops God's blessings. But by receiving Jesus Christ our fellowship is no longer broken with God, but restored. By receiving Jesus Christ, we are redeemed from the curse of the law.

"Christ redeemed us from the curse of the law by becoming a curse for us, for it is written; "Cursed is everyone who is hung on a tree." Galatians 3:13

"There's one God and one mediator between God and people, the man Christ Jesus." 1Timothy 2:5

How to Yield

When I think of the Scripture "obedience is better than sacrifice" I think about how sacrifice means to give up something and how the word obedient means to obey. When we sacrifice, it could be in money, material things, or maybe even a part of us. Sacrifice and obedience do not necessarily always go hand in hand. Sacrifice represents that we acknowledge God but not that we are necessarily following what God is telling us to do.

Some may say, "I'm giving this up for lent" thinking their sacrifice may right a wrong they have done. Not to say that sacrifices aren't important because they are. But sacrifices should be something that we give because we love the Lord, because he loved us so much that he became the perfect sacrifice for our sin. It should make us not want to sin knowing that sin is what required the blood of Jesus to be shed in order to cleanse us from our sin. If we could give money or some type of sacrifice and feel it will waive a wrong, we are wrong. If that were the case, there would have been no need for Jesus who was our perfect sacrifice to die for our sin once and for all. It was because of Jesus love for us that Jesus was obedient even to death on the cross. It says in the Bible that obedience is better than sacrifice. Many people today are like the people in the Bible. They thought by going around and doing what they felt they had to do that they could give their sacrifices and didn't have to be obedient to God's word because their sacrifice would give them favor with God.

"There is a way that seems right to a man, but in the end it leads to death." Proverbs 14:12

"Through Christ Jesus the law of the spirit of life in Christ Jesus sets us free from the law of sin and death." Romans 8:2

In the Bible it says, "Sin shall not be the master over you." Romans 6:14

God doesn't want us to sin but since we aren't perfect if we do sin we have an advocate; Jesus Christ.

"This is the message that we have heard from him and declare to you: God is light; in him there is no darkness at all. If we claim to have fellowship with him yet walk in darkness, we lie and do not live by the truth. But if we walk in the light, as he is in the light, we have fellowship with one another, and the blood of Jesus, his son, purifies us from all sin. If we claim to be without sin, we deceive ourselves and the truth is not in us. If we confess our sins, he is faithful and just and will forgive us our sins and purify us from all unrighteousness." 1 John 1:5-9

Jesus commanded us to love Him first, to love even our enemies, and He said that if we loved Him; we would obey His commandments. This is how we know that we love the children of God: By loving God and carrying out his commands.

"This is love for God: to obey his commands. And his commands are not burdensome, for everyone born of God overcomes the world. This is the victory that has overcome the world, even our faith." 1 John 5:2-4 NIV

We have a new commandment which is to love as Jesus loved. By keeping this one commandment we fulfill all the other commandments given to stop sin.

"A new commandment I give to you, that you love one another; as I have loved you, that you also love one another." John 13:34 NKJ

"It is for freedom that Christ has set us free." Galatians 5:1

I've heard many people say, "There's nothing we can do, whatever is going to happen will happen."

The Bible says we can do something to make a difference. The Bible says we have not because we ask not. James 4:2

A lot of people say we're in the last days, there's nothing we can do.

The Bible says "If my people, who are called by my name, will humble themselves and pray and seek my face and turn from their wicked ways, then I will hear from Heaven and will forgive their sin and will heal their land." 2 Chronicles 7:14 NIV

Maybe your mountain is sickness, maybe your mountain is a financial need. If you are a believer you have rights that have been given to you and as you continue to read the Bible you will discover great benefits that you can enjoy on earth as well as benefits that are out of this world.

Jesus said "If you have faith the size of a mustard seed, you can say to this mountain, "Move from here to there' and it will move. Nothing will be impossible for you." Matthew 17:20

Maybe your mountain is sickness, maybe your mountain is a financial need. If you are a believer you have rights that have been given to you and as you continue to read the Bible you will discover great benefits that you can enjoy on earth as well as benefits that are out of this world.

God's Wonderful Miracles

When I had my first child I was not a believer. I had a very hard time with the labor of my first born. My doctor was very old fashioned and said it was better for the baby's health if I didn't have anything for the pain, so I didn't. The pain was unbearable; I was in labor for 18.5 hours. But thank God the result was a healthy beautiful baby girl, Jennifer Rose Finley weighing in at 9.5 lbs. She was born naturally and was naturally the most beautiful baby girl ever born.

The doctor had a problem with the placenta not coming out so he pushed on my stomach a few times and his problems were over. I'll never forget it. A one pound placenta flew out and hit him right in the face. It was a little embarrassing but it was funny.

He walked out of the delivery room with blood all over his clothes laughing and with a loud voice, saying, "I just got hit by a flying placenta". At least the painful delivery had a funny ending. I heard so many people say you tend forget about the pain after the joy of seeing your child and holding it. It wasn't the case with me. I was afraid to have any more children.

When my husband saw what a terrible time I had with our first he said he was so sorry and wouldn't let this happen again. Of course as time went on, he seemed to forget how bad of a time I had with our first. He begged me to please try again for a boy. We tried and I became pregnant right away, but unfortunately in my fifth month I had a miscarriage, a boy. It was very hard. I couldn't understand why. I was very hurt.

We were told that sometimes a miscarriage was just natures' way of taking care of things. I was devastated. I spent Christmas in the hospital. Though it was a very difficult time for me, I got through it. People held me up in prayer and they encouraged me to try again and said that it would be alright. A year passed by and I became pregnant again. We were so happy and believed it would be different this time. A friend of mine knew my situation and she gave me some powerful Scriptures to read that pertained to pregnancy. These Scriptures and confessions were targeted at having childbirth with no pain and having a healthy pregnancy, quick labor, smooth delivery, and speedy recovery. I made sure that I read them faithfully every day.

I learned that pain in childbirth was a curse found in Genesis 3:16

I Timothy 2:15 says women will be saved from the pain of child birth if they believe.

In the book of Galatians 3:13 it states that Jesus redeemed us from the curse of the law, and now that I received Jesus Christ I was redeemed from that curse. I continued to read the Scriptures and speak the confessions/promises that belonged to me. At first it seemed hard to believe because our minds are so used to thinking natural, and to think it's only natural to have pain in childbirth. But I had been down that road before and decided I'd rather believe in the supernatural this time. To know I wouldn't have to have pain in childbirth made me excited and happy about trying again. I read the Scriptures and prayed the prayers over the baby and myself. As I read the Scriptures daily, my faith grew stronger. They really helped me to believe.

As the Bible says, faith comes by hearing the word of God. I prayed everyday for a healthy baby, and thanked God that I was redeemed from the curse and that I would not have pain and I would have a healthy pregnancy, easy labor and delivery as well as a fast recovery. It was amazing!

I started going into labor, and I started to feel pain but I would immediately pray in the spirit and it would immediately subside. With my first child tears continually rolled down my face from the pain, though I didn't make a sound. There was no way I was able to talk during the labor because of the pain being so intense. This time, I could talk to people during the labor and delivery. It was so amazing! The world would say I had the baby naturally because nothing whatsoever had been administered to me for pain. I know I had the baby supernaturally by the power of God! We thanked God for a healthy baby boy weighing in at 10 lbs, 9.5 ounces. Of course he was the most handsome boy that had ever been born, Kirk Douglas Finley. Because of his large birth weight, ice packs were used to reduce the swelling that I had incurred. It was so amazing though, I had no pain from it! We were the talk of the hospital. The nurses and doctors were amazed at how I didn't have any pain and didn't need pain pills or anything. Our God is an awesome God! When nurses came in they said I can't believe you had him naturally. I said, "I didn't, I had him supernaturally."

I hope this true story will encourage you to trust in the Lord also. God is not a respecter of persons, what he does for one, he'll do for another. Some people may say, "Well, you must be special."

I thank God that I am but God sees all of his children as special. When you think about it, it's like a will. If someone left a will and you were in it, but you didn't have knowledge of it how could it benefit you? In the same way you can compare God's word (the Bible).

God's' word is his will. When we receive Jesus Christ, we are joint heirs. We legally are entitled to all the promises contained in it. But if we don't read it and find out what it says and believe it and take it for our self it doesn't benefit us. As the Bible states,

"My people are destroyed because of the lack of knowledge." Hosea 4:6

I'm so thankful that Jesus Christ redeemed me from the curse.

"Let the redeemed of the Lord say so." Psalm 107:2

The Choice to Obey

We have a choice. We can choose life or death.

Another one of the curses are sicknesses and diseases as are listed in the book of Deuteronomy 28-30. God specifically says: "I have set before you life and death, blessing and cursing; therefore choose life, so both you and your descendants may live; that you may love the Lord your God, that you may obey his voice, and that you may cling to him, for he is your life and the length of your days. The Lord your God will make you abound in all the work of your hand, and will bless you with good health, as well as bless you financially."

If we choose to disobey God the opposite can happen, curses can come upon you: Sickness, poverty, failure, etc.

Faith Comes By Hearing the Word

I remember one day when my cousin heard there was a special meeting going on at a church in Wheaton. She invited me because they were praying for people who were sick and I needed healing. She said if you have faith to believe that you could be healed. I said I don't know if I have enough faith to believe it. I felt unworthy; I was a new believer and was just learning about the things of God. I had a growth the size of an orange on my fallopian tube and it was causing a lot of pain and problems in my body. I went to a couple different doctors. One said I should have surgery right away. I went for a second opinion and the last doctor said he was afraid to open me up. I was given medicine but it wasn't helping.

At first I felt those unworthy thoughts, like, I should be glad that I can talk and that I can walk. There are people much worse off than me. After I listened to the minister speak for a little while, I started feeling faith rise in my heart because he said everything I needed to hear. He talked about how God wants you healthy, how it's his will. "If you don't want the blessings of God, I'll take them," he said.

As I heard God's word spoken, "Beloved I wish above all things that you prosper and be in health, even as your soul prospers." 3 John1:2

Doubt left and faith came into my heart.

He also mentioned other Scriptures from the Bible pertaining to how much God loves us and wants only good things for his children. It happened, just as the Bible says:

"Faith comes by hearing the word." Romans 10:17

Faith came into my heart, and I knew it was God's will for me to be healthy. I am the Lord that heals you. Exodus 15:26

My husband and my cousin's husband were with us but they were not believers. They were very skeptical about God healing and then I went up to the front to be prayed for.

In the Bible it says, "These signs will follow those who believe, they shall lay their hands on the sick and they shall recover." Mark 16:18

As soon as the minister placed his hand on my head, I felt a warmth flow through my body. I actually felt emptiness on my right side where the growth had been. It was supernaturally removed by the power of God. Then afterward my husband told me something very interesting, he said that at the same moment I felt the power of God move within me; my husband said he also felt something in the same effected area in him. It reminded us about the Scripture that says we become one flesh when we are married. It made him start to think.

I went home and felt fine. I didn't have any more pain or problems from then on. I also had a doctor do an ultrasound and there was no longer any growth in my body to be found. I didn't go up for prayer for my back, but when I was a teenager someone had pulled a chair out from under me and I had permanent damage to my tailbone. It caused major problems through out my life. Many times I had problems trying to straighten up if I sat down on a bench, etc. I couldn't help but notice that after that day of prayer, my back was also healed. It never bothered me at night again or any other time!

I was so thankful! Since my husband lived with me, he could see the change in me after being healed. God showed him. It definitely got him to thinking.

CHAPTER 13

Laugh and Live

Laughing is very important; it should be on your list of things to do in case you forget about it. We really should make a point of laughing regularly. When I see some people going through their day and seeing they need to lighten up, I try to make them laugh or at least smile and sometimes the smile turns into a laugh. I remind them that "Life's too short to be too Serious" That's my motto and I'm sticking to it. Just as we take our supplements, we should take laughing as seriously. If you don't see humor around you, then do what you need to do. Find people that make you laugh and hang around with them. Find a funny book or a movie. Look at the person next to you. Laugh at your circumstances, laugh at yourself.

Laughter's Benefit
I love to laugh and it's so nice to be free to do so. It feels good to laugh and not only does it feel good

but it actually has a lot of benefits that I thought were pretty amazing. The next few pages will give you proven medical facts on how laughter benefits you. Have you ever heard someone laugh and you had no idea what they were laughing about but they were laughing so freely that it became contagious and caused you and others to laugh also? I love it when that happens.

I remember when I used to care about what people would think if they heard me laugh. I remember when I didn't think it was possible to feel like laughing unless I had a few drinks. It's so wonderful to know that's there's more. It's so great to be so free that I don't care anymore if someone hears me laughing.

In my past, I used to feel like I should hold laughter in but now I'm completely free. It's so nice to not have to be drunk with wine but be filled with the spirit as the Bible says. Ephesians 5:18

The Bible says that God will fill us with joy in his presence. Psalm16:11.

Ain't Nothing Like the Real Thing

The joy you receive from being in the presence of the Lord does not compare to any drink or drug. I know because I've been there. Remember that song? Ain't nothing like the real thing baby, Ain't nothing like the real thing. Well, there ain't.

I like to spend a lot of time in the presence of the Lord and the Bible says in the presence of the Lord there is fullness of joy. Since the result of joy is usually laughter, it makes it very easy for me to laugh. Joy and peace go hand in hand and it's a lot better combination than gin and tonic or rum and coke.

Lord, I remember when I thought that the love, joy and peace that I found in you were too good to be true. I'm so thankful that I was wrong.

If you've been looking for love in all the wrong places, look no more, read on and you'll find it in the right place.

Laughter is good for your heart according to a University of Maryland Medical Center Study. "Laughter along with an active sense of humor may help protect you against heart attack, according to a new study by cardiologists at the University Maryland Medical Center."

Proverbs 17:22 states that a merry heart does good like a medicine, but a broken spirit dries the bones. As you see science and the Bible agree!

"She is clothed with strength and dignity; she can laugh at the days to come." Proverbs 31:25 NIV

"Sarah said "God has brought me laughter, and everyone who hears about this will laugh with me". Gen 21:6

Some people might have cried having a baby at Sarah's' age but she laughed and named her son Isaac which means laughter. Consider that she was ninety years old and her husband Abraham was nearly one hundred years old.

"He will yet fill your mouth with laughter and your lips with shouts of joy." Job 8:21

"Our, mouths were filled with laughter, our tongues with songs of joy, then it was said among the nations, The Lord has done great things for them. Psalm 126:2 NIV

"There is a time to weep and a time to laugh." Ecclesiastes 3:4

Studies on the Powerful Effect of Laughter

"Laughter is a powerful medicine. It can lower stress, dissolve anger, and unite families in their resolve to overcome troubled times." —University of Nebraska"

When we laugh, natural killer cells can destroy tumors and viruses and release along with them a disease fighting protein.

The Science of Laughter Discovery health website states, "As well as lowering blood pressure, laughter increases oxygen in the blood, which also encourages healing."

According to Texas A & M University, "Humor can positively influence a person's state of hopefulness and reduce stress.

The sound of roaring laughter is far more contagious than any cough, sniffle or sneeze.

Laughter relaxes the body and reduces problems associated with high blood pressure, strokes, arthritis, and ulcers.

A good healthy laugh can reduce stress, lower blood pressure, elevate mood, boost immune system, improve brain functioning, protect the heart, connect you to others. Laughter can foster instant relaxation and make you feel good.

Laughter increases the chemistry of the will to live and increases our capacity to fight disease.

Historically research has shown that distressing emotions, depression, anger, anxiety, and stress are all related to heart disease."

A study done at the University Maryland Medical Center suggests that a good sense of humor and the ability to laugh at stressful situations helps mitigate the damaging physical effects of distressing emotions.

Humor improves brain function and relieves stress. Laughter stimulates both sides of the brain to enhance learning.

It eases muscle tension and psychological stress, which keeps the brain alert and allows people to retain more information.

Laughter gives our bodies a good workout. Laughter can be a great workout for your diaphragm, abdominal, respiratory, facial, leg, and back muscles.

It massages abdominal organs, tones intestinal functioning, and strengthens the muscles that hold the abdominal organs in place.

Not only does laughter give your midsection a workout, it can benefit digestion and absorption functioning as well.

It is estimated that hearty laughter can burn calories equivalent to several minutes on the rowing machine or the exercise bike.

Humor improves brain function and relieves stress.

Laughter gives our bodies a good workout.

Humor is a powerful emotional medicine that can lower stress, dissolve anger, and unite families in troubled times. Mood is elevated by striving to find humor in difficult and frustrating situations.

Humor changes our biochemical state. Laughter decreases stress hormones and increases infection fighting antibodies. It increases our attentiveness, heart rate, and pulse.

Humor also helps us avoid loneliness by connecting with others who are attracted to genuine cheerfulness.

And the good feeling that we get when we laugh can remain with us as an internal experience even after the laughter subsides.

Laughing at ourselves and the situation helps reveal that small things are not the earth-shaking events they sometimes seem to be.

Humor changes behavior – when we experience humor we talk more, make more eye contact with others, touch others, etc.

Increases Energy

Humor increases energy, and with increased energy we may perform activities that we might otherwise avoid.

Our work, marriage and family all need humor, celebrations, play and ritual as much as record-keeping and problem-solving.

A healthy sense of humor is related to being able to laugh at oneself and one's life.

Laughing at oneself can be a way of accepting and respecting oneself.

Lack of a sense of humor is directly related to lower self esteem.

Note that laughing at oneself can also be unhealthy if one laughs as a way of self degradation.

Humor is essential to mental health for a variety of reasons:

Humor helps us replace distressing emotions with pleasurable feelings. You cannot feel angry, depressed, anxious, guilty, or resentful and experience humor at the same time.

Lacking humor will cause one's thought processes to stagnate leading to increased distress.

Humor changes behavior – when we experience humor we talk more, make more eye contact with others, touch others, etc.

We should ask the questions "Do we laugh together?" as well as "Can we get through this hardship together?

Humor binds us together, lightens our burdens and helps us keep things in perspective.

One of the things that drain our energy is the time and focus we put into coping with life's problems including each other's limitations.

Our families, our friends and our neighbors are not perfect and neither are our marriages, our kids or our in-laws.

When we laugh together, it can bind us closer together instead of pulling us apart.

Remember that even in the most difficult of times, a laugh, or even simply a smile, can go a long way in helping us feel better.

Laughter is the shortest distance between two people.

Humor unites us, especially when we laugh together. Laughter heals.

It is not situations that generate our stress; it is the meaning we place on the situations.

Humor adjusts the meaning of an event so that it is not so overwhelming.

Mental health professionals point out that humor can also teach perspective by reality rather than the distortion that supports their distress.

I pray that you take these words about humor to heart and decide to laugh more as a way of looking at life from a different perspective.

Chapter 14

Free from Fear

What is fear? According to Merriam Webster dictionary:

1. Fear in oneself worry, anxiety, and terror.

Remember it's not of God to be gripped with fear.

"God did not give us a spirit of fear, but of power and love and a sound mind." 2 Timothy 1:7

"For you did not receive a spirit that makes you a slave again to fear, but you received the spirit of son ship. And by him we cry, "Abba, Father"

Romans 8:15

2. A reverential awe; fear of God

Fearing God doesn't mean that we should feel the way an abused child does in the presence of a raging parent.

The reverent and worship and fear of the Lord is the beginning and the principal and choice part of knowledge its starting point and its essence; but fools despise skillful and Godly wisdom, instruction, and discipline.

3. To be afraid of: expect with alarm. This is a good fear, more of a natural fear if it warns us as to prevent a danger that lies ahead.

An inward feeling of caution.

Unhealthy fear is fear that controls us and consumes us. The best way to deal with this fear is to replace it with faith.

"And faith comes by hearing and hearing by the word of God."

Romans 10:17

I remember how there had been times in my past when I had been changing TV channels and came across a channel that gave me a bad feeling. Instead of changing the channel, I let my curiosity get the best of me. Then I would feel bad and regret it later and repent. I now know better than to watch those things that are contrary to the word because it will have the opposite effect. Those bad thoughts were planted in my mind which even years later affected me at times. I would feel fear grip me, and be reminded of something terrible I had seen in a movie. I know that it was because I yielded my self to that spirit of fear.

Overcoming Crippling Fear

There were times that I felt such extreme fear that it overpowered me to the point that I felt afraid to be alone in my house after my husband had left the house early in the morning for work. I wanted to beg him to stay home, that's how afraid I felt. There were other thoughts along with terrible feelings that some-one may break in and try to kill me or attack me. It was terrible and I realized that I needed to read the Word more and to be wise to the enemy by not watching bad things that would try to instill fear.

Fear is real and a lot of people have had real prob-lems as the result of opening themselves up to that spirit of fear. Problems such as nervous breakdowns, committing suicide, and drug and alcohol addictions are some of the causes that fear has produced. Fear of failure, low self esteem, guilt, shame, the spirit of fear is all behind it. It makes you afraid of what people may think.

The Bible says it's better to be pleasing to God than to people. There were other times where the spirit of fear tried to make me afraid to leave my house. If I hadn't had the knowledge that it was a spirit of fear that makes you afraid and if I hadn't had the understanding that the greater spirit lived in me I may have been one of those people that succumbed to the fear and its consequences. God's word clearly states that fear is a spirit. "God has not given us a spirit of fear, but of power, and love, and a sound mind." 2 Timothy 1:7

My True Counselor

Some people have asked if I had been to coun-seling or if I had to take medication or if I presently take medication due to what I had been through. The answer is no.

The Lord has been my counselor and he sent his word and healed me. Through other's prayers and my own time in the word and in prayer I received strength and healing. But spending time in praise and worship has been where I truly found the help I needed. In his presence is where we become strong. I'm not saying that there's anything wrong with going to counseling or taking medication, I'm just answering the question that many have asked. "For unto us a child is born, unto us a son is given: and the government shall be upon his shoulders: and his name shall be called Wonderful, Counselor, The mighty God, The everlasting Father, and The Prince of Peace." Isaiah 9:6

"Where the spirit of the Lord is there is freedom." 2 Corinthians 3:17 NLT

"It is for freedom that Christ has set us free." Galatians 5:1 ESV

Speaking God's word is powerful: Say "Thank you Father that you've not given me a spirit of fear, but of power and of love and of a sound mind"
2 Timothy 1:7

It's clear that fear is a spirit but that it's not of God. God gives us a spirit of power of love and a sound mind.

As you say God has not given me a spirit of fear, but of power and of love and a sound mind and as you believe it and mediate on it, you will have victory over the fear. Perfect love casts out all fear. God is love.

"Do not fear, for I am with you; do not be dismayed, for I am your God. I will strengthen you and help you; I will uphold you with my righteous right hand." Isaiah 41:10

Free of Fear

Whatever your fear may be, you can be free from it. Maybe you have a fear of failure, maybe a fear of death, maybe a fear of a sickness that you were told runs in your family. When you become a part of the family of God, it changes everything. You become free. The law of the spirit of life in Christ Jesus sets you free from the law of sin, sickness and death.

When I made the decision to ask Jesus Christ to be my Savior and started reading the Bible, I was so excited to learn that it's a fact that I no longer have to accept fear and depression.

The Bible makes it clear that fear is a spirit, but when you have Christ, you have power to overcome fear.

The Bible also makes it clear that depression is a spirit and the Bible says put on the garment of praise for the spirit of heaviness which is depression. Isaiah 61:3

"You, dear Children, are from God and have overcome them, because the one who is in you is greater than he that is in the world." 1John 4:4

I was so thankful to find out that Jesus paid the price for my freedom, that I could finally be free and stay free.

God's love is key, "God's perfect love drives out all fear." 1 John 4:18

"There is no fear in love, but perfect love casts out fear; because fear has torment. He that fears is not made perfect in love." 1 John 4:18

"The Lord is my light and my salvation-Whom shall I fear?" Psalm 27:1

"When I am afraid I will trust in you." Psalm 56:3

"I sought the Lord and he heard me and delivered me from all my fears"- Psalm 34:4

I remember being at my grandma's house on my wedding day. As I was looking in the mirror to put on my veil, my aunt said, "Debbie, it's not too late to change your mind." I'm so glad that I didn't listen to fear.

That was 32 years ago and I'll never regret it. I thank God for it everyday. In the Bible it says to build your house on the rock, Jesus Christ, and it will stand. There's no power on this earth that can stand against God's word.

I'm so thankful that God's word is the truth and that his truth prevails.

After we accepted Christ we started learning how we were not each others enemy.

The Real Enemy
The Bible says we do not fight against flesh and blood but against principalities, against powers, against the rulers of the darkness of this world, against spiritual wickedness.

The devil tries to convince us that we are each other's enemy, by putting thoughts in our mind to play us against each other.

We need to know that our enemy is not each other, and when couples who are married have come to the true understanding, they will have a blessed marriage that will continue to grow stronger every day.

I'm reminded of the song, "What's love got to do, got to do with it?" God is love and his love has everything to do with it. It was God's love for us that gave us his only son Jesus Christ. He died for us that we might have eternal life through his blood that he shed for us on the cross.

It was because of Jesus love for us that Jesus was obedient even to death on the cross.

"Greater love has no one than this that he lay down his life for his friends." John 15:13 NIV

Human love can be selfish, and human love can fail, and come to an end. The God kind of love never ends and is perfect.

"A new commandment I give unto you that you love one another; even as I have loved you. By this all shall know that you are my disciples, if you have love one to another." John 13:34

God's love is the greatest power there is. God's love never fails. 1 Corinthians 13:13

Jesus said we are to walk, even as he walked. If we walked even as he walked we would walk in the love and power of God and avoid strife and contention.

According to God's word we don't have to accept a lot of things any longer. We can have power in our life by applying God's word. Instead of the devil continuing to have control over us, we can live in a higher realm.

Jesus said in the word that he would give us power over all the power of the enemy. Luke 10:19.

"According to the Bible the thief comes to kill, steal, and destroy." John 10:10

One of those ways is by bringing the spirit of strife or division, etc. to steal our peace and destroy our relationship.

We learned the importance of immediately repenting and forgiving. If we walk out of love, since the Word teaches us, it actually commands us to love one another; we are giving place to the devil by walking out of love. John 13:34

Learn to Forgive Right Away

One day, I was tempted to hold a grudge against my husband for something my husband had said or done. I don't actually remember what had happened but the Lord reminded me that we're to walk in love, and that it is a command. I had walked out of love by not forgiving him right away,

And then God began to help me see that it was to my advantage and to Kirk's to forgive immediately. When we walk out of love for another person, we are walking out of God's will and if we're not in his will, we walk out from under his protection.

Though it may sound funny, I pictured what it would be like holding hands with the devil instead of my husband and that by walking out of love, that's what we're really doing.

The thought disgusted me so much that it helped me to become quick to forgive and repent. Not only that but how it was sin to walk out of love, and how it was sin that nailed Jesus to the cross to begin with. I remember when I thought it was just an expression never go to bed angry but it actually is a Scripture in the Bible. "In your anger, do not sin. Do not let the sun go down while you are still angry." Ephesians 4:26 NIV

Before I had accepted Christ, there would be times when we didn't talk to each other for a whole day, maybe even two days for petty things. This was thirty years ago. It's good to know who your enemy is. "Be sober and self controlled. Be watchful. Your adversary, the devil, walks around like a roaring lion, seeking who he may devour." 1 Peter 5:8

Now we know better than to allow the devil to use up our precious time. Also the Scriptures make it clear that when it appears that people are doing us wrong, that really spirits are influencing people to work against us.

Just as God brings people into our lives to bless us, the devil can use people to do the opposite.

"For we are not wrestling with flesh and blood contending with only physical opponents but against powers, against the master spirits who are the world rulers of this present darkness, against the spirit forces of wickedness in the Heavenly supernatural sphere." Ephesians 6:12

"Be strong in the Lord, be empowered through your union with him; draw your strength from him, that strength that his boundless might provides." Ephesians 6:10.

"Put on God's whole armor, the army of a heavy armed soldier which God supplies, that you may be able successfully to stand up against all the strategies and deceits of the devil." Ephesians 6:11

When we dwell in the secret place of the most high we abide under the shadow of the almighty, he covers and protects us. Psalm 91

We are commanded to love one another and it is for our own good. God is love and when we walk out of love, we walk out from under the protection of God. John 13:34

Neighborhood of Love

When we walk out of love, we walk into the enemy's territory it's kind of like going into a bad neighborhood, but in a spiritual sense. The Bible says not to give place to the devil, because you are then subject to danger versus protection. You can very well be robbed spiritually, of your peace, joy, and health.

As mushy as it seems, now Kirk and I miss each other each day, we go to work, looking forward to seeing each other at the end of each day.

We look forward to hearing each others voice on the phone each morning and at lunch time.

We are so thankful that we not only have human love, but a supernatural love from God also, because human love can be selfish. But the God kind of love is the greatest power. It never fails and it grows. Sounds too good to be true but I'm glad it's not.

I've always liked the illustration of the triangle:

The bottom two corners are you and your mate. The top corner of the triangle is God.

If you draw closer to God, you will automatically draw closer to each other, and if you draw closer to each other, you will automatically draw closer to him and find "The joy of the Lord is your strength." Nehemiah 8:10

The power to overcome

There were many times in my life that I was gripped with fear, and I had good reason to be. But even when I didn't have a good reason the spirit of fear and depression that used to control my life would come back to try and buffet me even as an adult. When I made the decision to ask Jesus Christ to come into my heart and started reading the Bible, I was so excited to learn that it's a fact that I no longer have to accept fear and depression.

The Bible makes it clear that fear is a spirit, but when you have Christ, you have power to overcome fear.

Also the Scriptures tell us to put on the garment of praise for the spirit of heaviness (depression) and as you enter into praise and worship, it will clothe you with power and strength.

Praise will drive away the spirit of heaviness and you will experience joy, because in his presence there is fullness of joy and the joy of the Lord is your strength. God's word is full of power: "As we speak and hear his word (the Bible) faith will come by hearing the word" Romans 10:17 "Just as negative words can tear us down, positive words can build us up. But God's word is more than just positive, it's full of power and it doesn't return void. "As the rain comes down and the snow from the sky and doesn't return there, but waters the earth and makes it bring forth and bud, and gives seed to the sewer and bread to the eater, so shall be my word that goes forth out of my mouth: It shall not return to me void, but it shall accomplish that which I please, and it shall prosper in the thing whereto I sent it." Isaiah 55:10-11

Fearless Love

"God is love, and he who dwells and continues in love dwells and continues in God, and God dwells and continues in them." 1 John 4:16 Amplified

Later in my life since my father didn't live a Christian life, I questioned whether he had a relationship with the Lord. Since my grandma was a godly person and my dad met me at my grandma's house on Sundays, I knew she had a lot of opportunities to talk with him. I started to feel really bad about the thought of him not making Heaven. Then all of a sudden I was reminded of the day when my father was murdered. I remembered how at that same moment that he was shot, our glances met. There was no fear in his eyes and wondered how it was possible. Well, the Lord reminded me of the

Scripture, "Perfect love casts out all fear. God is love." My question was answered.

"There is no fear in love, but perfect love casts out fear; because fear has torment. He that fears is not made perfect in love." 1 John 4:18

"Where the spirit of the Lord is there is liberty." 2 Corinthians 3:17

"It is for freedom that Christ has set us free." Galatians 5:1

"Fear of man will prove to be a snare, but whoever leans on, trusts in, and puts his confidence in the Lord is safe and set on high." Proverbs 29:25 Amplified

"God can and will restore if you only believe and trust in him." Joel 2:25

"It is better to trust in the Lord than to put confidence in people." Psalm 118:8

Human love usually is a love that is based on feelings and emotions that can change from one moment to the next but God loves you with an unconditional love. His love never changes. He loves you with an everlasting love.

Chapter 15

Control Your Destiny

So many of us can look back and see that we are at this place and time in our life because of choices and decisions that were made in our life. You alone can control your destiny; the choice is up to you, because you are a person with a free will.

The most important decision in life which determines your eternal destination can be made right now.

The Bible says, "Now is the time, choose life while there's still time, tomorrow may be too late. Man is like a breath. His days are like a shadow that passes away." Psalm 144:4

It's God's will that you choose life. "It's the Fathers heart desire that all would be saved and come to the knowledge of this truth." 1Timothy 2:4 NIV

God didn't make us like robots; he made us individual people that have a will to make choices because he's a just God.

You may say, "I believe in God, the devil believes in God also and Hell is his destination."

If this seems strong it is meant to be because there is a Heaven to gain and a Hell to shun. Jesus is the bridge.

Jesus said, "I am the door; no one can come to God, except through him."

Our Life ... is but a Vapor

God says that our life is but a vapor. For what is your life? It is even a vapor that appears for a little time and then vanishes away. James 4:14

Our life on earth is a short time especially compared to eternity.

Eternal life is everlasting. And this is the record that God has given us eternal life, and this life is in his son. Those that have the son have life and those who do not have his son do not have life. 1 John 5:11-12

There is life and death before you. Choose Life!

Jesus said, "I am the way, the truth, and the life; there is no life outside of me."

"Ask and it will be given you; seek and you will find; knock and the door will be opened unto you" Matthew 7:7 NIV

"You will seek me and find me when you search for me with all your heart." Jeremiah 29:13 NIV

If you were to breathe your last breath right now, do you now where you would go? You were created in the image of God, meaning you are a spirit being because you were created in God's image, a spirit lives forever, either in Heaven or in Hell.

The choice is up to you. It's God's will that all would come to know him.

As we look around in our life, as well as other peoples lives we can see how uncertain life can be. Especially with everything that's happening around the world today.

You never know what tomorrow holds.

"As the Bible says, Life is like a vapor, here today, gone tomorrow." James 4:14

It was Jesus' love for you that held him on the cross that day.

So many people's lives were snuffed out, though they were healthy and young. No one is guaranteed a tomorrow. If you put your faith and trust in God, your future will change, it's certain as the dawn. God commended his love toward us, while we were yet sinners, Christ died for us. Jesus could have called down ten thousand angels to rescue him from the cross.

But he loved you so much that he chose death on the cross that we might have eternal life through him by believing and receiving him.

It was Jesus' love for you that held him on the cross that day.

If you will say with your mouth the Lord Jesus and believe in your heart that God raised him from the dead, you will be saved and set free from the curse.

For with the heart one believes unto righteousness, and with the mouth confession is made unto salvation.

If you'll notice, the Scripture doesn't say that we are to believe in our minds that Jesus is Lord. Mental assent is not good enough.

Also, Lord means master, Christians have been bought. "You are not your own, for you have been bought with a price" 1 Corinthians 6:19-20

"The price was the precious blood of Jesus" Hebrews 9:22

Receive God's gift of love; salvation through his only son, Jesus Christ.

Start a New Life Right Now

You can start a new life in Christ by repeating this prayer:

Father, I thank you for sending Jesus to die on the cross for my sins.

Thank you Father God, that you raised Jesus from the dead that I may have eternal life through him.

I ask you Jesus to forgive me of my sins. I receive you as my Lord and Savior.

You gave your life for me, and I now give my heart and life to you because you loved me so much.

Thank you, Jesus, that if I breathe my last breath, I have a guarantee that my eternal destination is eternal life in Heaven.

Thank you that I have been redeemed by the blood of Jesus, and that I'm redeemed from the curse.

When you call to him he will listen to you and you will seek him and you will find him when you search for him with all your heart.

"Jesus said, I assure you most solemnly I tell you, that unless a person is born again anew from above he cannot ever see know, be acquainted with and experience the kingdom of God." John 3:3

When a person becomes a Christian, they are "born again". They have a new birth and new life in Jesus Christ. It's a spiritual rebirth. Christian means Christ like, it is not a religion, and it's a way of life, through a personal relationship through Jesus Christ.

"If anyone is in Christ, they are a new creature: old things are passed away; behold all things have become new." 2 Corinthians 5:17

CHAPTER 16

There's Such Power in Praise!

Praise means "to commend, applaud or magnify" Webster defines the word praise as to say good things about and it is synonymous to words such as admire, commend, extol, honor, and worship. A definition of Christian praise is the joyful thanking and adoring of God.

Choose to have a Good Day

Some people wonder what kind of day they're going to have and think that getting out of the wrong side of bed has something to do with it. We can choose to have a good day in spite of our circumstances because when you live in the higher realm that the Lord has made available for you to walk in there's power that goes with you.

If you want to start out your day right, as soon as you get up in the morning, Say Good Morning to God, or Hello. Thank him for the day he made. Thank him for his love. Some people aren't here any longer, you are. Thank him, rejoice and be glad. You have a choice. A lot of times we may not feel like it but if we do, whether we feel like it or not, it will cause our feelings to change for the better and you will feel like it as a result.

If we abide in him and he abides in us and since he is love and his love is the greatest power there is God will reign in our life through Jesus Christ. "Through Jesus, therefore, let us continually offer to God a sacrifice of praise- the fruit of lips that confess his name." Hebrews 13:15

"Enter into his gates with thanksgiving and into his courts with praise. Be thankful to him, and bless his name." Psalm 100:4

Praise lifts us into God's presence so we can rise above our circumstances.

You can choose to yield to a spirit of heaviness which is depression or you can choose to be free from it. By putting on the garment of praise for the spirit of heaviness you will find freedom.

There's actually a Scripture that says put on the garment of praise for the spirit of heaviness—Isaiah 61:3

There were many times that I had dealt with a spirit of heaviness. I'm so thankful for the power that comes down from Heaven as we praise and worship God. The Spirit of The Lord is great and mighty.

"You dear children are from God and overcome them, because the one who is in you is greater than the one who is in the world." 1John 4:4 NIV

- First of all, he's so worthy of our praise.
- Second, he inhabits our praises.
- Third, in his presence is fullness of joy.
- Fourth, the joy of the Lord is our strength.

David Learns Praise

As you see David in Psalm 59:16-17, it shows that David started out each day by worshipping God and singing aloud, which resulted in him being clothed in power and strength. The garment of praise was something that he put on and we can put it on also which will clothe us in power and strength.

David learned that power is released when we worship God, even in the midst of trouble.

We can learn a lot from David. Psalm 119:164 tells us that David praised God seven times a day. He is a great example to follow.

We can have an intimate relationship with God also. As we continue to spend more time praising and worshipping God daily, it will enable us to have God's strength, peace and power flowing in our life daily.

Wherever we are, we can praise the Lord, just as thankfulness can be an attitude of the heart and is so important, so is praise. As we drive, walk, shop, clean the house, or even lay in bed. "I will bless the

Lord at all times: his praise shall be continually in my mouth" Psalm 34:1

"Though you have not seen Him, you love Him; and even though you do not see Him now, you believe in Him and are filled with an inexpressible and glorious joy." 1 Peter1:8

"Since God inhabits our praises, that means our praising God brings down his presence." Psalm 22:3

"In the presence of the Lord there is fullness of joy." Psalm 16:11

"The joy of the Lord is your strength." Nehemiah 8:10

The joy that you can experience from being in the presence of God doesn't compare to anything else.

"Then make my joy complete by being like-minded, having the same love, being one in spirit and in purpose." Philippians 2:2

Praise stills the enemy. Praise lifts us into God's presence so we can rise above our circumstances.

"Whoever offers praise glorifies me and to him that orders his conduct aright I will show the salvation of God." Psalm 50:23

As you come to understand how much God loves you and how much he longs to have time with you, you will long to have more time with him. As we draw near to him, he draws near to us.

Praise is a sacrifice, we may not always feel like it, but God understands that we are human. Even David had to make himself praise at times when he didn't feel like it. In Psalms, David said bless the

Lord, O my soul, I've been reminded of that and then would tell my soul, bless the Lord O my soul, and then go off into praising God. God honors your faith and obedience.

"By him therefore let us offer the sacrifice of praise to God

Continually, that is, the fruit of our lips giving thanks to his name"Hebrews13:15

Jesus is Worthy of Praise

People all over the world praise people for hitting a ball or kicking a ball during sport's games. Jesus did a lot more than make a homerun or a touchdown. He bought us with his blood. He paid the price in full for our eternity. All we have to do is accept his free gift.

Jesus is so worthy of our praise!

Because of his love for us he suffered a terrible death on the cross, he is so deserving of our thanks and praise for what he's done for us.

It's pleasing to him when we bless his name, and when we bless him, he blesses us back. It's a win win situation.

"Draw near to God and he'll draw near to you" James 4:8

God manifests his power through praise.

One way to praise him is to sing to him. Psalm 33:3

Another way of praise to God is lifting up your hands to him, lift up your hands in the sanctuary, and bless the Lord. Psalm134:2

Another way is by praising him with an instrument.

Psalm 150:4 Praise brings peace:

Another way is to be still: "Commune with your own hearts upon your bed and be silent." Psalm 4:4 Amplified

Praise Honors God. "He who sacrifices thank offerings honors me." Psalm 50:23

Praise brings freedom physically as well as spiritually.

In the Bible there's a story of Paul and Silas that were unjustly put in prison and at midnight they started praising God which resulted in an earthquake that shook the prison and the doors flew open to free them. Acts 16:25-26 NIV

Praise brings protection. It protects your mind, body and spirit.

"But let all who take refuge in you be glad; let them ever sing for joy. Spread your protection over them, so those who love your name may rejoice in you." Psalm 5:11

As you praise God, his blessings flow into your life.

Praise Brings the Presence of God

Praise brings the presence of God on the scene.

Praise stills the enemy. The story in the Bible explains how the children of Judah found themselves outnumbered by the armies of Ammon, Moab and Mount Seir. God told them he would do the fighting for them.

The people of Judah being the people of praise that they were, knew that God manifests his power through praise, the power of God showed up since God inhabits the praise of his people and the victory was theirs. 2 Chronicles 20:22

Praise brings glory to God which is most important but in return you can receive healing, deliverance, strength, peace, and refreshing. Many times during praising and worshipping God I've been set free from the spirit of heaviness, and even headaches.

In the Bible when people were depressed, they were delivered through praising and playing instruments unto God.

That still works today, there is such power in praise. Praise stills the enemy.

"I know the thoughts that I have towards you says the Lord, plans of peace and not of evil, to give you a future and a hope." Jeremiah 29:11-13

As you continue on your journey in life seeking God in prayer and reading the Bible you will find strength to help you in your time of need.

Scriptures of Praise

Here are some more great Scriptures to feed your spirit and mind:

"The Lord is my strength and my shield; my heart trusts in him, and I am helped" Psalm 28:7 "My heart leaps for joy and I will give thanks to him in song." NIV

"As you keep your mind on Jesus he will keep you in perfect peace, a peace that passes all understanding that the world can't give you." Philippians 4:6-7

"You will show me the path of life; in your presence is fullness of joy; at your right hand are pleasures forevermore." Psalm 16:11

"The Lord is far from the wicked but hears the prayers of the righteous." Proverbs 15:29 NKJ

"The memory of the righteous is blessed." Proverbs 10:7 NKJ

I pray that this book has helped you to see the truth. "Then you will know the truth and the truth will set you free." John 8:32 NASB

"Delight in the Lord and he shall give you the desires of your heart" Psalm 37:4

"But from everlasting to everlasting the Lords love is with those who fear him, and his righteousness with their children's children." Psalm 103:17

"The blessing of the Lord makes us rich, and he adds no sorrow with it." Proverbs 10:22

"For the kingdom of God is not a matter of eating and drinking, but of righteousness, peace and joy in the Holy Spirit." Romans 14:17

Simple Ways to Have a Great Life

1. " Do not forget my teaching, but let your heart keep my commandments."

2. "For length of days and years of life and peace they will add to you."

3. "Do not let kindness and truth leave you. Bind them around your neck; write them on the tablets of your heart."

4. "So you will find favor with and good repute in the sight of God and man."

5. "Trust in the Lord with all your heart and do not lean on your own understanding."

6. "In all your ways acknowledge him and he will direct your path." Proverbs 3:1-6

"Oh magnify the Lord with me and let us exalt his name together." Psalm 34:3

"Deborah sang and praised the Lord after defeating the Canaanites." Judges 5

"Rejoice always, pray without ceasing, and in everything give thanks; for this is the will of God in Christ Jesus for you." 1Thessalonians 5: 16-18 NKJV

"You are a chosen generation, a royal priesthood, a holy nation, his own special people that you may proclaim the praises of him who called you out of darkness into his marvelous light." 1 Peter 2:9 NKJV

"Let everything that has breath praise the Lord." Psalm 150:6 NIV

"Oh, that we would praise the Lord for his goodness, and for his wonderful works". Psalm 107:8

Remember that God loves you with an everlasting love.

Remember we love him because he first loved us. To know him is to love him. Remember that as you come to know him more you will experience more love and power in your life. Your peace and joy will increase resulting in a brighter future. Embrace the truth, it is life changing. Remember, you can learn to live and walk in a higher realm of life.

Debbie, her Mother, and half brother

Gene feeding a squirrel

Debbie and her two half brothers

Debbie in her Fire Truck

Debbie with her Grandpa (Mothers Father)

Grandma (Mothers mom) and half brother

Debbie and her Mother in law (Sally)

Her son, Kirk and his cousin Jamie

Debbie with her daughter Jennifer in Athens, Greece

Jennnifer with her Great Grandpa in Thessalonica, Greece

Son (Kirk) with Great Grandpa in Thessalonica, Greece

Grandpa & Debbie in Thessalonica, Greece

Debbie and her husband, Kirk

Kirk with their children, Cheri, Jennifer and Kirk

Destined To Marry

Debbie at age 3

Kirk at age 10

About The Author

Deborah K. Finley is a freelance writer and author and was born and raised in Chicago with a heart to help hurting people.

"What Your Future Holds and what you Can Do to Change It," is her first book. She has also contributed to other anthologies, which include "Praise Reports-January 2007" and "How I Met My True Love" both books published by Xulon Press.

She's an Illinois Certified Domestic Violence Professional and speaks at women shelters, churches, etc. She has earned her PhD from SHK School of Hard Knocks. She resides in Island Lake, IL, with her husband, Kirk. They have served as worship leaders for many years, and are doing so presently at Good News Christian Center in Des Plaines, IL. She and her husband are also students of New Life Bible College.

God has put a passion in their hearts to spend time in praise and worship on a daily basis, and have found that there's no better place to be, because as we draw nearer to God he draws nearer to us.

God has shown them his faithfulness over and over again, watching over his word to perform it.

Deborah and Kirk both have a longing in their hearts to help others to experience the life changing presence of God in their own lives.

Just as the Bible says:

God inhabits the praises of his people. In the presence of the Lord there is fullness of joy, and the joy of the Lord is our strength!

God has been continually opening doors for them to minister in testimony and song. They are thankful to God for the privilege and honor of calling them.

Deborah was inspired to write this book because she did not foresee having a future. From a childhood that threatened to destroy her, to a teenager that was an eyewitness to her fathers' murder, she survived supernaturally. She had a life changing encounter that transformed her future from darkness to light and wants you to know that this power is made available for you today so you can learn to live in a higher realm of life!

Endnotes

Enright, R. D., & Zell, R. L. 1989. Problems encountered when we forgive one another. *Journal of Psychology and Christianity, 810, 52-60.*

Freedman, S. R. 1998. Forgiveness and reconciliation: The importance of understanding of how they differ. *Counseling and Values, 42, 200-216.*

Freedman and Enright 1996 wrote: When one forgives one does not open a jail cell door.

Enright, R. D. 2001. *Forgiveness is a choice: A step-by-step process for resolving anger and restoring hope.* Washington, DC: American Psychological Association.

University of Maryland Medical Center-Laughter is good for your heart 2000

Texas A & M University 2000 Humor can positively influence a person

Laughter is a powerful medicine- University of Nebraska 2001

Laughter lowers blood pressure- Science of Laughter Website 2001

"LOVE CAME DOWN" by Lenny LeBlanc and Lindell Cooley

© 2001 Integrity's Hosanna! Music/ASCAP & LenSongs Publishing/ ASCAP & Music Missions Publishing/ASCAP c/o Integrity Media, Inc., 1000 Cody Road, Mobile, AL 36695 & LenSongs Publishing, Inc. 800 County Road 27, Florence, AL 35634 & Music Missions Publishing, address unknown.

Editor: Julie Dearyan

To contact Deborah Finley:
What Your Future Holds
P.O. Box 781 Island Lake, Il. 60042
E-Mail: info@whatyourfutureholds.com

Website:
www.whatyourfutureholds.com

Please include your prayer requests, comments
or help received from this book.

Warning: Side Effects

Warning! This is a book that contains powerful words that are not only natural but also supernatural. These words are full of power that can affect your life in a positive way.

They can be life changing as you read and meditate on them. These words are not mere words, as in a newspaper, but these words are spirit and life.

As you read this book with an open mind and open heart your life can be transformed!

You can become prosperous and have good success by meditating on the word day and night so you may be careful to do everything written in it.

According to world report's, words are falling out of people's mouths daily and seeping into others minds. But do not be conformed to this world but transformed by the renewing of your mind.

Dosage: Day and night, read regularly even though it may not seem to have any effect at the start.

Avoid alcohol and recreational drugs. They will interact with it badly.

Main cause: Calming effect, A peace that passes all understanding that the world can't give you, comfort, wisdom, so you can be wiser than your enemies, keen insight, discernment, better health, strength, so you can soar on wings like eagles, so you can run and not grow weary, and walk and not be faint, you may experience laughter from so much joy so use caution when operating heavy machinery or driving.